THE BREATH OF REGENERATION

Its Power, Its Presence, and Its Motivation

by

Rev. Dr. Kenneth J Harrell Sr.

DORRANCE
PUBLISHING CO
EST. 1920
PITTSBURGH, PENNSYLVANIA 15222

Dorrance Publishing Co
585 Alpha Drive
Suite 103
Pittsburgh, PA 15238
Visit our website at *www.dorrancebookstore.com*

ISBN: 978-1-4809-4057-4
eISBN: 978-1-4809-4080-2

This book will foster a stronger relationship with God in understanding his divine power from which the breath of God provides Regeneration power to His creations.

To those who have inspired me to reach for a higher level of education and spiritual meaning, which was by the grace of God reached just because of Him.

Jehovah Head Trinity
Ms. Geneva Harrell Spurgeon, Mother
Mrs. Denese J. Sander Harrell, wife
Mrs. Dyanna Williams, soldier
Mrs. Hetty Tavernier
Rev. Dr. Cora L. Smithson, Dean, Central Bible Institute
Rev. Dr. Odessa McNeill, Dean, Eastern Bible Institute

Acknowledgments

This book was first written as my thesis for a doctoral in theology. I was so blessed to have attended The Central Bible institute in Piscataway, New Jersey, under the leadership of Dr. Cora L. Smithson, Dean, and with the assistances from Dr. Odessa McNeill, Academic Dean for the Eastern Bible Institute, Irvington, New Jersey; and the Doctoral Staff of the Freedom Bible Institute.

Through their obediences and God's given vision, I was provided the opportunity to reach such heights of academia. This book is a reflection based on my personal experiences as I continue to grow in spirit and while watching the reactions of others Saints of God who were just coming out of storms in their lives as members of the body of Christ Jesus.

My prayers are continually for the three churches I have been blessed to attend on my return home from retirement from the armed forces. First, my home church, Sharon Baptist Church of New Brunswick, New Jersey, under the leadership of Rev. Conway L. Johnson, Jr.; second, the Community Baptist Church of North Plainfield, New Jersey, under the leadership of Rev. James M. Robinson; and finally, the Bright Hope Baptist Church of Montclair, New Jersey, under the leadership of Rev. Charles H. Kelly (retired), for their love of Christ Jesus and the wisdom they provided to me at my times of need.

My life path began with Him, and it was sequestered to develop a personal relationship with Him. I, like all of His creations, am to lift up praise unto Him. Like all other new beginners, I was unable to fully understand the nuance of His words, but by His divine grace and blessing for me, He added in the ingredients of hope and wisdom and a desire to learn more each day. His grace, mercy, hope, and wisdom, mixed with my prayers, are the tools I used to guide me to travel through and reach the other side of the many storms past, and those to come storms that would have destroyed the hopes and aspirations of the old me.

There are many positive driving forces in my life, but the first human inspiration comes from a mother, Geneva Harrell-Spurgeon, who obtained a lower level of education yet set the bar high in education for her children.

I would be remiss to not acknowledge the brothers and sisters who helped me develop a sharper spiritual values and deeper principles that yielded a closer relationship to the deity of the Trinity of God.

I would like to thank those family and friends who, without fear, sat down, read chapters, and offered constructive criticism.

CONTENTS

INTRODUCTION

My desire is to show how the topic "The Breath of Regeneration: Its Power, Its Presence, Its Motivation" has a profound effect on the practices of worship under the sovereignty of God, His grace and mercy for those who are disobedient as demonstrated by Adam and Eve, creation, and residents of God living in the Garden of Eden.

In his work titled, Basic Studies in Soteriology, Mr. Allen suggests that our original parents, who were created by God, Adam and Eve, were created with three elements. From the dust was Adam's body formed, a soul was given, and the Holy Spirit (the breath of God). These factors are as described by Mr. Allen reasons why they were given the ability to hear, walk, and have dialogue with God. His next statement influenced me in formulating a thesis statement that defines the true divineness of God's nature and the fervent works of the Holy Spirit.

Mr. Allen's next sentences inspired me to question their accuracy, which helped me to develop a hypothesis statement. He suggests, "Something happened in the Garden of Eden that resulted in our fore-parents losing one of the three elements. The one divine element which connected them to God and was the one element which allowed them to have fellowship and companionship is the Holy Spirit."

Our Father, who is in Heaven, set the tone for all fathers of the world to emulate. He loved his creation, Adam and Eve, which he consistently demonstrates just as he demonstrated his love to us on a daily basis. Like our earthly fathers, when we demonstrate disobediences we are subject to some form of discipline. My interpretation of the scripture implies that God disciplined Adam, Eve, and the serpent. This is done to deter bad behavior and also to show his genuine love for his creations. The serpent, which beguiled Eve, was cursed to eat the dust of the earth for the rest of his life. "15: And I will put enmity between thee and the woman, and between thy seed and her seed; it shall bruise thy head, and thou shalt bruise his heel. 16: Unto Eve God commanded that he will greatly multiply thy sorrow and thy conception; in sorrow thou shalt bring forth children; and thy desire shall be to thy husband, and he shall rule over thee. 17: And unto Adam he said, because thou hast hearkened unto the voice of thy wife, and hast eaten of the tree, of which I commanded thee, saying, Thou shalt not eat of it: cursed is the ground for thy sake; in sorrow shalt thou eat of it all the days of thy life" (Genesis 3:15-17, KJV).

God, the creator of heaven and all that is within and without, still demonstrated love for Adam and Eve. Found in verse 21: "Unto Adam also and to his wife did the Lord God make coats of skins, and clothed them. God questioned the curiosity of the newly developed mind of Adam and Eve speaking of the dangers of them venturing to the tree of life and consuming its fruit which would give them eternal life" (Genesis 3: 22). Banning them was the second form of a disciple and thirdly a way of securing the future of mankind.

THE BREATH OF GOD

In the first book of the Holy Bible, Genesis chapters 1, 2, and 3, we read the story of how God created heaven, earth, and man in his own image. 1 Genesis 1:27: "So God created man in his own image, in the image of God created he him; males and females created he them." 2 Genesis 2:7: "And Lord God formed man of the dust of the ground, and breathed into his nostrils the breath of life; and man became a living soul." As we read further we see that the creation of Eve was conducted by the first medical operation performed by God." Genesis 2:21: "As Adam was placed into a deep sleep as one of his ribs was removed and God created Eve and God brought her to Adam who announced that she was bone of his bone and called her woman, because she was taken out of man."

In Genesis 2:24-25, we are introduced to our first parents' wedding ceremony, which also was performed by God. 24: "Therefore shall a man leave his father and his mother, and shall cleave unto his wife; and they shall be one flesh. 25: And they were both naked, the man and his wife, and were not ashamed."

The key word used to support my thesis is found in Genesis 1:27: "And God breathed into his nostrils the breath of life." I feel that Mr. Allen forgot who was doing the creating. The definition of breath as found in Webster's New Collegiate Dictionary, is "air filled with a fragrance or odor, an act of breathing, a slight breeze, air inhale and exhaled in breathing, spirit, animation, to draw in oxygen and give out carbon dioxide through natural processes, to blow softly, to send out exhaling, to instill by or as if by breathing a new life into the movement." God breathed into the nostrils of Adam the breath of life, and the second creation of man was completed in the image of God. God's breath, which bears his power, brings life Adam inhaled his pure air of life, not the polluted air that is in our atmosphere today God exhaled his divine spirit into man unlike his creation of the living creatures of the heavens and earth and those that are in the depths of the sea by speaking those things into existences. Adam received life as air filled his lungs. He began to move, his eyes opened, and he awakened, looking into the glory of God, and God called him man.

Genesis 1:1-5 states: "In the beginning God created the heaven and earth. 2: And the earth was without form, and void; and darkness was upon the face of the deep. And the Spirit of God moved upon the face of the waters. 3: And God said, 'Let there be light': and there was light. 4: And God saw the light, that it was good: and God divided the light from the darkness. 5: And God called the light day and the darkness he called night. And the evening and the morning were the first day." Matthew Henry's commentary of the whole Bible Volume I, Genesis to Deuteronomy points to the first article of our creed that God the Father Almighty is the maker of heaven and earth, and as such we believe in him.

The effect produced the heavens and the earth, that is, the world, including the whole frame and furniture of the universe, the world, and all things therein (Acts 17:24). The world is a great house, consisting of upper and lower stories, the structure stately and magnificent, uniform and convenient, and every room well and wisely furnished.

In the visible world, God's breath is easy to observe: 1. Great variety, several sorts of beings vastly differing in their nature and constitution from each other. Lord, how manifold are thy works, and all good. 2. Great beauty, the azure sky and verdant earth are charming to the eye of the curious spectator, much more the ornaments of both. 3. Great exactness and accuracy. 4. Great power, it is not a lump of dead and inactive matter, but there is virtue, more or less, in every creature: the earth itself has a magnetic power. 5. Great order, a mutual dependence of being, an exact harmony of motions, and an admirable chain and connection of causes. 6. Great mystery, there are phenomena in nature that cannot be solved, secrets that cannot be fathomed or accounted for. But from what we see of heaven and earth, we may easily enough infer the eternal power and Godhead of the great Creator, and may furnish ourselves with abundant matter for his praises.

2

With the creation of the heaven and earth, which God spoke into existence, we are adorned still with secrets, beauty, and will remain in his grace and mercy. With such beauty adorning the heavens, why would God create man? Why would God place in the hands of man all of his creations just for man to exploit others with earth's natural resources? This question was addressed by Mr. Wayne Grudem, author of the book *Systematic Theology*. He notes "in chapter 11 the discussion of God's independence, we note several Scripture passages that teach that God does not need us or the rest of creation for anything, yet we and the rest of creation glorify him and bring him joy." Since there was perfect love and fellowship among members of the Trinity for all eternity (John 17:5, 24), God did not create us because he was lonely or because he needed fellowship with other persons; God did not need us for any reason.

Nevertheless, God created us for his own glory. In our relationship with him, he created a conscience in us that speaks right or wrong, creating a well of independence. Note that God speaks of his sons and daughters from the ends of the earth as those "whom I created for my glory" (Isa. 43:7; cf. Eph. 1:11-12). Therefore, we are to "do all to the glory of God" (1 Cor. 10:31).

So if God created Adam and Eve for his glory, they who were given life by the breath of life have been banned from his presence and they last communication with him. God has demonstrated even in the creation period that his love superseded all others. All was created by the spoken Word of God. God inhales a breath of air and while exhaling it back into the atomosphere, the third person of God, the Holy Spirit converted change into. "He breathes into the nostrils the breath of life." Eve was created by means of an operation. Once all parts were in proper order, God sat back and announced, "It is good." He breathed also the breath of life into Eve's nostrils and she lived. Her lungs were filled with his breath. There was movement. She opened her eyes to meet her creator and was escorted by God to meet her husband.

Man and woman, both of God's creation, are now filled with the Holy Spirit, The body, the soul, and the Holy Spirit are actively in harmony with the regeneration power of God. God so loved his creations, they were placed in a heavenly Garden surrounded with all of God's wonders and splendors, the tree of life, of wisdom and healing, and a neverending flow of living water. For man, who was placed in a land with such splendor and beauty, there still remained a warning that demands care. Warning of the dangers of the tree located in the center of the Garden that it would bring death.

⸺◇⸺

Nothing Is Lost on the Breath of God

Nothing is lost in the breath of God,
Nothing is lost forever;
God's breath is love, and that Love will remain,
Holding the world forever.
No feather too light, no hair too fine,
No flower too brief in its glory;
No drop in the ocean, no dust in the air.
But in counted told in God's story.
Nothing is lost to the eyes of God
Nothing is lost forever.
No journey too far, no distance too great,
No valley of darkness too blinding;
No creature too humble, no child too small
For God to be seeking, and finding
Nothing is lost to the heart of God
Nothing is lost forever;
God's heart is love, and that love will remain,
Holding the world forever.
No impulse of love, no offices of care,
No moment of life in its fullness;
No beginning too late, no ending too soon,
But is gathered and know in God's goodness.
Words and music (c) Colin Gibson 1994

MAN'S FIRST SIN
THAT CAUSED SPIRITUAL DEATH

Satan used the serpent to clothe himself to tempt Eve by getting her to doubt God's instructions and warning. He implied that God was a strict disciplinarian for not wanting Eve to share his knowledge of good and evil. Satan made Eve forget all that God had given her, and instead she focused on the one thing she should not have. Disobedience opened their eyes, and with knowledge of both good and evil it resulted in a disastrous outcome.

Mr. Allen stated, "They died spiritually, immediately as God confronted them about the matter." Spiritual death is defined as a second death; it's a death of the soul or, more generally, a death in the afterlife. Dr. John B. Calhoun, author of the book Death Squared; the Explosive Growth and Demise of a Mouse Population, saw the social breakdown of a population of men given simple resources as a second death. He saw this as a metaphor for the potential fate of man in an overcrowded but resource-rich environment and made reference to the second death in the book of Revelation. In Christian theology, spiritual death is defined as a spiritual separation from God, brought on by sin. Christians believe that spiritual death and physical death were brought into the world through the fall of man.

"You must know, then, let the maidens who have chosen to live a godly life learn through you, that there is a death of the soul, though by nature the soul is immortal." This is made clear by the beloved disciple Apostle John, the theologian, when he says, "There is sin that leads to death and there is sin that does not lead to death" (1 John 5:16, 17). By death he certainly means "here is the death of the soul." Apostle Paul says, "Worldly sorrowfulness produces death" (2 Cor. 7:10), certainly of the soul. Again, Apostle Paul says, "Awake, you who sleep, and arise from the dead, and Christ shall give you light" (Eph. 5:14). From which enjoined to arise? Clarity, from those who have been killed by sinful desires that wage war against the soul (1 Pet. 2:11). Hence the Lord also described those who live in this vain world as dead, for when one of His disciples asked to be allowed to go and bury his father, He refused permission and told him to follow Him, leaving the dead to bury their dead (cf. Matt. 8:22). Here, then, the Lord clearly calls those living people dead, in the sense that they are dead in soul. The separation of the soul from the body is the death of the body, so the separation of God from the soul is the death of the soul. This death of the soul is the true death. This is made clear by the commandment given in paradise, when God said to Adam, "On whatever day you eat from the forbidden tree you will certainly die" (cf. Gen. 2:17). And it was indeed Adam's soul that died by going through his transgression, which separated him from God, for bodily he continued to live after that time, even nine hundred thirty years (cf. Gen. 5:5). The purpose of God in forbidding them to eat this fruit was to test their obedience and to manifest his authority as Lord. As viewed by God and measured by his law, man was guilty of unbelief, gross ingratitude, inordinate pride, ambition, and unnatural rebellion, most deliberate and far reaching, murder. Total depravity accrued by this one sin, man completely severed his allegiance to God, for which disobedience, the favor and communion of God was withdrawn, and war introduced into the soul itself.

St. Gregory Palamas suggests that death, however, befalls the soul because transgression not only crippled the soul and made accursed; it also rendered the body itself subject to fatigue, suffering, and corruptibility, and finally handed it over to death. For it was after the dying of his inner self brought about by the transgression that the earthly Adam heard the words "Earth will be cursed because of what you do, it will produce thorns and thistles for you; through the sweat of your brow you will eat your bread until you return to the earth from which you were taken: for you are earth, and to earth you will return" (Gen. 3:17-19).

OMNIPRESENCE IS HE

Let's look at the definition of the word "Omnipresence" as stated from Webster's New Collegiate Dictionary: "Omnipresence as a noun; it is defined as the quality or state of being omnipresent, Omnipresent as an adjective is defined as being present in all places at all times. Omnipotent is defined as one who is omnipotent; God." The definitions provided just gave the basic meaning of Omnipresence, Omnipresent, and Omnipotent. There must be an understanding of the divine powers held upon our God, our redeemer Jesus Christ, and the Holy Spirit. As found in Dake's Annotated Reference Bible, we find a definition that is more in line with the direction I am headed. "11: We find the following; Omnipotent; means all power" (Rev. 19:6). God's infinite power must be sensibly understood as operating within the bounds of His own revelation of Himself. According to Scripture, God has limited Himself to working within certain limitations in some realms. Perhaps it is not so much a question of what he could possibly do, but what He morally allows Himself to do. The example given by the author points to the fact that God cannot lie (Tit. 1:2; Heb. 6:18), which means that He is absolutely truthful and can be depended upon, unlike man; He is above lying. Morally it's impossible for Him to lie. He formed the heaven and the earth by breathing words of creation from His lips. His powers are such that if He desires to permit himself to do so, He can and will not. For that reason alone, it is declared that He cannot lie.

Omnipresent means "everywhere present." In his book; Dake introduces the three persons in the Godhead: God the Father, Jesus Christ the Son of God, and the Holy Spirit. The Old Testament has provided scripture to support their existence. In Genesis chapter 1, we find God creates the heaven and earth. He creates man in His image. The Word of God is God's Son Jesus, who comes from heaven into this world, clothed Himself with human skin; He distances Himself from the Father and the Holy Spirit to live here. After His resurrection and ascension back unto the presences of the Father, He's now seated at the right hand of the Father. He waits for permission from the Father to return as He explained to His disciples for His final harvest.

The Holy Spirit; He is spoken of as moving upon creation (Gen. 1:2), coming into the midst (2 Chr. 20:14), descending from heaven unto Jesus after His baptism in the form of a dove (Mt. 3:16, Mk. 1:10; Lk. 3:21-22), and abiding with or departing from men (Jn. 14:16, 26; 15:26; 16:7-11).

Omnipresence—or ubiquity, then—is different from Omni-body and is governed by a relationship and knowledge of God. Like the presence of someone being felt by another who is thousands of miles away. So it is with the presence of God among men (1 Cor. 5:3-4).

With a greater knowledge of the truth that works within and around our God, we see his attributes as being the fundamental and necessary qualities of his nature that form the grounds for his various manifestations to his creatures. There are two general classes of God's attributes, which are absolute and relative. Absolute attributes means those that reveal and affect the inner being of God and His relation to himself, independent of his relation to the universe. Relative attributes means those that relate or reveal the outward relation of God to the universe, which he has made. God's absolute attributes are spirituality, infinity, self- existence, immutability, unity, truth, love, and holiness; His relative attributes are eternity, immensity, Omnipotence, veracity, Omniscience, omnipresence, mercy, and justice. With those factors implanted, we now can see why God loved Adam and Eve so much that he dressed them with animal fur before banning them outside the Garden of Eden.

Did they lose communication with God? My answer is yes, and yet I can also report no. Why? Because of their disobedience, they did lose their spiritual guide, the Holy Spirit, which was the breath of God inside them that became inactive, or dormant. My question is based on the facts that God's grace and mercy still remained with them even while outside the Garden of Eden. Mr. Allen suggests that we, the offspring of Adam and Eve, have lost fellowship companionship, or understanding of God or things pertaining to God until He chooses to regenerate a person and restore that spiritual element within us.

After Adam and Eve ate that forbidden fruit, they must have thought for many years that Satan may have been right in his statement they would not die a physical death. Death did not occur immediately after eating the forbidden fruit, but Adam lived to the age of nine hundred years old. But in God's own time they did die, which proves God's promise will be kept, always in his own time and purpose.

I faithfully believe that God's love for them, in his divine absolute attributes, followed his creations outside the Garden of Eden, watching over them like a loving father who has given his son or daughter blessings and permission to move out of the family home into their own apartment. He would drive by each day to check on them to see if things were progressing well.

We have already ventured into the definition of Omnipresence, Omnipresent, and Omnipotent, and agreed that they are the property of being present everywhere. According to Eastern Theism, God is present everywhere. We also agree that divine Omnipresent is thus one of the divine attributes of God, although in Western Theism it has attracted less philosophical attention than such attributes as omnipotence, or being eternal.

Dr. Richard Boeke writes in his article "Servetus, Science and the Breath of God," that in most religions, "Breath is a metaphor for God. Breathe on me, let the breath of God fill me with life anew." This statement is announced by many church under-shepherds while preaching from the pulpit while addressing the subject of salvation. It underlines the three major faith factors that help a new individual to make the decision about the saving grace of the salvation of Jesus Christ, and through the acceptance of Jesus' birth, death, and resurrection, who is now sitting at the right hand of the Father in heaven as the truth and light of the world.

The gift of the Holy Spirit is not endowed after baptism, but only by the divine will of God a person can receive this gift through prayer and fasting. As a social worker, I counsel individuals who are facing personal problems, storms, which are hindrances to their spiritual growth and development. I met and interviewed one individual who fellowships with a small group of men.

Growth Time Ministry is where a few men who have common life experiences, such as time in prison, drugs, and alcohol problems, and have demonstrated low social skills, come together to share on common ground to give testimony of how after finding Jesus their lives have changed. Their conversations, their testimonies consist not just of the surface issues but the deep-down stuff that causes death and brings to birth generational problems that affect themselves, their families, and communities—problems only God and Jesus would see when they are invited into our hearts.

We, like Adam, did eat of the forbidden fruit, and through its outcome it has affected our lives. One session I began our discussion on the topic based on the gift of the Holy Spirit. Larry, a six-foot African-American male who served ten years in state prison, responded that after his baptism he was under the impression that the Holy Spirit was immediately given after the submerging and raised from the water. He reported, "I found it strange that I felt some difference but I wanted the Holy Spirit that brings you to your feet; shouting and praising God without shame." Larry continues to report that he fasted and prayed daily for this gift from God.

While at work as a chef cooking breakfast for tenants at a nursing home, he was going through his daily routine. He was listening to Gospel music while scrambling eggs. He began to praise God in song, thanking him for another day when he felt the Spirit of God fall on him. He began to shout and praise God in the kitchen. He reported burning the eggs and causing a mess. Larry was already regenerated by God, and just like the day of Pentecost, when suddenly there comes a sound from heaven as of a rushing mighty wind. For Larry the presence of God was near, and his breath on him, the gift of the Holy Spirit. "14: And when the day of Pentecost had fully come, they were all with one accord in one place. And suddenly there came a sound from heaven as of a rushing mighty wind, and it filled the entire house where they were sitting. And there appeared unto them cloven tongues like as of fire, and it sat upon each of them. And they were all filled with the Holy Ghost, and began to speak with other tongues, as the Spirit gave them utterance."

The Holy Ghost came to Larry while he was in one spirit with God, praising and glorifying God. The breath of God still lives. Pentecostals and some proponents of baptismal regeneration believe the Holy Spirit is something different from above and beyond, the saving "indwelling of the Holy Spirit." In an attempt to demonstrate this, they'll often argue that the Apostles received the Holy Spirit well before Pentecost. Thus, they insist, the baptism in the Holy Spirit, which they experienced at Pentecost, must be something different from, something more than, the receiving of the Holy Spirit, which they already experienced. This is, in fact, not the case, as the Word of God demonstrates. In the language of theology, "regeneration" is that decisive spiritual change, affected by God's Holy Spirit, in which a soul, naturally estranged from God and ruled by sinful principles, is renewed in disposition, becomes the subject of holy affections and desires, and enters on a life of progressive sanctification, the issue of which is complete likeness to Christ.

To which this word corresponds occurs only twice in the New Testament (Matthew 19:23-24): "Then Jesus said to His disciples, 'I assure you: it will be hard for a rich person to enter the kingdom of heaven! 24 Again I tell you, it is easier for a camel to go through the eye of a needle than for a rich person to enter the kingdom of God'" (Titus 3:5). He saved us not by works of righteousness that we have done, but according to His mercy, through the washing of regeneration and renewal by the Holy Spirit. And as the first instance denotes, not the renewal of the individual but the perfected condition of things at the "Parousia," the second coming.

In this verse in the book of Titus, this scripture speaks of the "washing of regeneration," which connects us to the renewing of the Holy Ghost with the ritual of baptism, as an outward symbol and seal.

Mr. Jame Orr in the book of Hasting Dictionary of the Bible informs us that the doctrine, nevertheless, is a thoroughly scriptural one, and the change is named by a great variety of terms and phrases: "born," "born anew," "a new creation," "renewed," and "quickened," to which attention will immediately be directed. The fundamental need will immediately be directed. The fundamental need of regeneration is recognized in both the Old Testament and New Testament.

Found in John 3:3; Jesus replied, "I assure you: Unless someone is born again, he cannot see the kingdom of God." Spiritual life, as it is taught, can come only from a spiritual source, and man naturally has not that life. Hence the declaration of the words "except a man is born anew, he cannot see the kingdom of God."

Life stories such as Larry's have been told by individuals whom God has called to His regenerated state. Please refrain from feeling that only males have given testimony of the saving grace of God. God has and still is calling for the regeneration changes from those who have been subdued by Satan's trickery, haven eaten the forbidden fruit. By the divine plan of God today and throughout the life of our Lord and Savior Jesus Christ, we have found forgiveness for our sins.

In the book by Linda Storm about the life of Karla Faye Tucker, titled *Set Free: Life and Faith on Death Row*, we find the life story of a young white female whose life choices placed her in prison for the murder of two people. A child of seven or eight years old, she was first introduced to drugs by her sister, who caught her smoking pot. In order to keep her quiet, she gave some to her. Karla talked of her experiences in school, of how other students' parents would ensure their children would stay away from her. She spoke of her first experience with heroin. She said that her sister's friends were in a biker club and one of them came to see her sister, who was not at home, and took her off on his motorcycle. He introduced heroin to her and asked if she wanted to shoot it. After shooting her fill, she became sick and he ended up dropping her off at some apartment. By the time Karla was in the seventh grade, she was heavily involved with drugs and she dropped out of school.

But before all of those events ever happened in her life, God had a different plan. Somewhere along the way, she talked her mother into letting her go to church with them. She recalls, "I think they must have been very conservative, because they wore something on their heads and had to wear dresses. We sat on the front row. At some point she was down on her knees and really praying in the Spirit. I thought, *What is going on here?* Everybody came and laid their hands on her. I don't remember doing anything wrong that night, but they never would talk to me again." After such an experience for a seven-year-old girl who, for her first time, was visiting a church of God, while on her knees praying she was experiencing a personal relationship with Jesus and they did not understand its meaning. God looked deep into her heart and saw the outcome of life, the storms that she would travel through, the souls she would reach, the praise she would render unto Him even while on death row. Her question was, why didn't they reach out to me? Why did they cut me off? Those questions are asked even today. I recall after my acceptances of Jesus Christ feeling the same. But as a man of God today, I find it very important that the Church has to become more involved in the development of those who are regenerated. We can't allow them to walk away from the Church and not return. We have to reevaluate our approaches to salvation and look at our personal intentions and relationship to God. Through the life of Karla, those who read her testimony have accepted a personal relationship with Jesus Christ and have found that peace of assurance in knowing him.

The Word Is Jesus

Jesus Christ, our redeemer, has taken on many forms. Just the thought of Him humbles the hardened heart as the Word of God became the Son of God, our high Priest, but in all reality Jesus is Love, the Word of God. Before we can even have a discussion of the word as being Jesus, we must first introduce the One and True God. Like Yahweh in the Old Testament, God the Father is also Lord of the cosmos. He reveals himself in numerous events like thunderstorms (Mark 9:7; John 12:29, KJV). All things are from him, through him and for him (Rom. 11:36; 1 Cor. 8:6). He is the prototype of created light and the source of all life (John 5:26; 1 John 1:5; Rev. 21:23). In him we live and move and have our being (Acts 17:28). He feeds the birds, clothes the grass, and guards the life of even the smallest creature (Matt. 6:26-30; 10:29). He is in all things and through all things, but he is also over and above all things (Eph. 4:6). He is not flesh, but spirit and the "Father of the Spirits" (John 4:24; Heb. 12:9; Isa. 31:3). He transcends all creation as ("el 'elyon"), "God Most High" (ho hupsistos) (Luke 1:35; 7:6; 6:35; Acts 7:48). He is ("el hashshamayim"), "God of heaven" (Rev. 11:13; 16:11), "Lord of heaven and earth" (Matt. 11:25; Acts 17:24), and Father of heavenly lights (James 1:17). He sits enthroned in heaven as ("el shadda)i," "God Almighty" (ho pantokrator), who is even now taking his great power in hand and beginning to reign (Rev. 4:6; 11:16; 15:3; 19:6). Our Father is the King of ages, immortal, invisible, the only wise God (1 Tim. 1:17), a sovereign Lord (despotes) upon whom we may call in times of distress (Acts 4:24; Rev. 6:10). He transcends time as (el olam), the everlasting God (ho aionias thos) (Rom. 16:26). He is the Alpha and Omega, "who is and who was and who is to come, the one who lives forever and ever" (Rev. 1:8; 10:6). Finally, He is a living God who made the heaven and earth and the sea and all that is in them (Acts 14:15; 4:24; 17:24; Rev. 4:11) (passism). Fear God and give him glory, for the hour of his judgment has come, and worship him who made heaven and earth, the sea and the fountains of water: these are the words of the everlasting Gospel, that John heard proclaimed in his vision on the island of Patmos (Rev. 14:7). God the Father is truly the ultimate focus of our worship and the final end of all history (1 Cor. 15:24-28; 1 Tim. 1:17; Jude 25).

Yahweh, the God of Israel, is the Father of the Word, which is Jesus Christ. He hath in these last days spoken unto us by his Son, whom he hath appointed heir of all things, by whom also he made the worlds. The many authors of the old and new testaments they proceeded to highlight the difference between the prophets and Jesus by noting two unique aspects of Christ's identity. First, Jesus is naturally the Heavenly Father's heir because Jesus is God's Son. Since God has only one Son (John 3:16), the Father's entire estate belongs to Christ Jesus and He doesn't have to divide the inheritance with anyone. This being the case, all things that God has also belong to Christ. No prophet could make such a claim, and certainly no prophet knew the Heavenly Father in the way that His own Son does.

Second, God created the physical realm through Christ. Many readers of the New Testament are familiar with John 1:1-5, which speaks of Christ as "the Word" regarding His role in creation. This builds on an ancient Jewish metaphor that uses God's word or wisdom as a symbol for His active, personal involvement in human affairs (Proverbs 8). First-century Jews believe that God engages and influences through His divine Word, which essentially signifies His personal will and created the physical universe (God said, "Let there be"). It was by His Words that everything was made.

But that view is incomplete without Jesus. As the eternal Word who "was with God" and "was God" (John 1:1), Christ is the one through whom the Father made everything; thus Jesus was actively involved in our world from the very beginning, not just when He came to earth. With understanding that Jesus Christ, before electing to become flesh, helped in the creation of the heaven and earth, creating all things large and small, the Word of God even accompanied God in the collection of dust, he even drew in the air used to breathe into the nostril of man who was brought to life. The Word of God even called on Adam and Eve after they hid from God. "2: Then the man and his wife heard the sound of the Lord God walking in the Garden at the time of the evening breeze, and they hid themselves from the Lord God among the trees of the Garden. So the Lord God called out to the man and said to him, 'Where are you?' And he said, 'I heard you in the Garden and I was afraid because I was naked, so I hid.' Then He asked, 'Who told you that you were naked? Did you eat from the tree that I commanded you not to eat from?'" (Genesis 3:10, KW).

The questions and answers were from God and Jesus as the living word conducted the examination. The Word of God was even at the trial of Adam and Eve; He was the one who announced the verdict of guilty and sentenced them to abandonment. Are Adam and Eve spiritualists? Are they allowed the forgiven grace of God through "Regeneration"?

Sandra D. Wilson, in her book, *Into Abba's Arms*, addressed the question hopefully you have developed within your spiritual mind. Has God abandoned Adam and Eve? In her article "Abandoning Grace," her question is, have you noticed that some supposedly Bible-believing churches and organizations can be very confusing? They talk and sing a lot about grace, God's unmerited favor toward sinners as the sole basis of right relationship with him. But the thrust of their teaching pictures a "booster rocket" kind of grace. Like Karla, she got the clear impression that grace launched them into Christ's life. But once they were in spiritual orbit, their relationship with God depended more on their righteousness than on Christ's. For Karla it blossomed while in prison, and for Sandra it occurred while she attended her local church. The measurement of righteousness was determined by how perfectly Sandra followed denominationally determined rules and regulations. For Karla, in prison life was based and determined on rules and regulations given by the State. Spiritually she developed her righteousness with God through the Chaplin services and the Word of God (the Bible). Tithing, reading the Bible rigorously, attending church, and avoiding specific sinful activities; for Sandra it was dancing, for Karla it was drugs and alcohol.

Sandra writes that she didn't know it at the time, but she was to control God's affections toward her by being good enough to keep her place of belonging in his family. For Karla, while in prison she understood that her experiences from her first church visit as a child, she could not hear or be filled with the Holy Spirit until she was healthy enough to inhale the breath of God as He comforted her with His soft, loving voice of God. Once in the grace of God, she remained.

The Apostle Paul certainly knew about the dangers of an abandoning kind of grace. He confronted the Jewish believers in Galatia, and Paul did not hold back any words found in verses 6 and 7 in the first chapter of Galatians. "22: I am astonished that you are so quickly deserting the one who called you by the grace of Christ and are turning to a different Gospel which is really no Gospel at all. Evidently some people are throwing you into confusion and are trying to pervert the Gospel of Christ." Sandra points to the word "Deserting." "It sounds a lot like abandoning to her. If we believe God's grace may abandon us, we will abandon God's grace. We'll desert, reject, and abandon grace, and we will substitute perfect keeping of the law as the way to be right (justified) before God." That's exactly what Paul told the Galatians they had done (Gal. 2:16; 3:6-14; 5:1-8). We as Christians have done the same thing.

But for Adam and Eve, they did not because their relationship with God was all they knew. Regulation, rules, and having a church relationship with God was lost by disobedience. God still provided his grace and did not abandon them.

REGENERATION, ITS POWER,
ITS PRESENCE, ITS MOTIVATION

Just what is "Regeneration"? "23: Regeneration is that act of God by which the government disposition of the soul is made holy, and by which through the truth as a means, the first holy exercise of this disposition is secured. 24: We believe that the Scripture teaches that in order to be saved, sinners must be regenerated, or born again; that regeneration consists in giving a holy disposition to the mind that is affected in a manner above our comprehension by the power of the Holy Spirit in connection with divine truth, as to secure our voluntary obedience to the Gospel; and that its proper evidence appears in the holy fruits of repentance and faith, and newness of life. 25: Regeneration is the act of God whereby He cleanses Gospel believers of the defilement of sin, renews their personhoods and the immaterial parts of their human natures (soul-spirit), and imparts to them spiritual life."

Calvinistic and Lutheran theologians regard regeneration as including the pre-salvation work of God in the sinner's heart as well as its completion in conversion. Regeneration consists of the inward renewal and impartation of spiritual life immediately following salvation faith in Christ (John 1:12-13; 3:16; 6:53). Though totally depraved, the sinner does not have to be regenerated to believe the Gospel since salvation faith is God's gift and has within itself the power to enable people to trust in Jesus (2 Peter 1:1; Acts 3:16). Any inclination of the heart toward God is a part of the Holy Spirit's pre-salvation work in drawing people to God (John 6:44). It means immediately following his salvation faith in Jesus, the Gospel believer is regenerated by the Holy Spirit (John 3:5-8; Titus 3:5), who works through God's Word.

From those definitions given, we agree that regeneration is rebirth. The phrase of "born again" is commonly used in the Baptist churches. What is regeneration, according to the Bible? "26: To be born again is opposed to, and distinguished from, our birth, when we were conceived in sin. The new birth is a spiritual, holy, and heavenly birth signified by being made alive. Our first birth, on the other hand, was one of spiritual death because of inherited sin. Man in his natural state is 'dead in trespasses and sins' until we are 'made alive' [regenerated] by Christ when we place our faith in Him" (Eph. 2:1). After regeneration, we begin to see, hear, seek after divine things, and to live a life of faith and holiness. Now Christ is formed in the hearts; we are now partakers of the divine nature, having been made new creatures. God, not man, is the source of this (Esp. 2:1, 8). It is not by men's works but by God's own good will and pleasure. His great love and free gift, His rich grace and abundant mercy, is the cause of it, and these attributes of God are displayed in the regeneration and conversion of sinners.

Nowhere in the Bible have we found that Adam and Eve were given the opportunity to experience a regeneration relationship with God. If we look at the creation of Adam from the dust of the earth and the one rib taken from Adam to create Eve including the divine breath of God, we can see that this divine act was their regeneration period. Regeneration is a part of the salvation package (Eph. 1:14), adoption into (Galatians 4:5), and reconciliation (2 Cor. 5:18-20). Being reborn from above is parallel to regeneration (John 3:6-7; Eph. 2:1; 1 Peter 1:23; John 1:1-13; 1 John 3:9; 4:7; 5:1, 4, 18). Regeneration is God making a person spiritually alive, a new creation, as a result of faith in Jesus Christ. Yes, the Word of God was present during the creation of heaven and earth. And yes, the Word of God acted as the prosecutor, Judge, and defense lawyer for Adam and Eve, but the regeneration and rebirth for them was not provided as it is applied to us this day. God still loved his creation and showered his grace and mercy throughout the lifetime of both Adam and Eve. The first family gift of salvation will continue to be a part of the Gospel as written in God's Holy Word (the Bible).

ITS PRESENCE

The power of regeneration; we are children of wrath (Eph. 2:3; Rom. 5:18-20). Before salvation, we are degenerated, but by God's grace after salvation we are regenerated. The power of regeneration can be explained as a transformation taken place within the person who is called by God. The first place affected would be the heart of the person. The impact of Christ's love, his redeeming power of salvation for us, enters into one's heart and ignites a divine reaction, which causes change. It moves and grows divinely in us for a period of time, continuously penetrating our hearts and minds, and once the mind and heart have been challenged we begin to see a newness, which effects our actions. During this period of transformation, we find the person is in a very fragile state because the storm's raging winds have subsided and they experience a peace that is so satisfying and pleasing it overcomes them. This is why I encourage a three-way partnership with the New Babe in Christ. This program places not only the Trinity, God the Father, Jesus Christ the Son, and the Holy Spirit, but it should also include the presence of a senior member of the Church who has demonstrated a strong relationship with God a man or woman who has demonstrated a strong prayer life, and who has withstood the mean storms of life, his family, and is well respected within his community and church. This attachment was first demonstrated by God as we read of the life transformation of Saul as he was on the road to Damascus. Saul, who was still breathing threats and murder against the disciples of the Lord, went to the high priest and asked him for a letter to the synagogues at Damascus, so that if he found any who belonged to the Way, men or women, he might bring them bound to Jerusalem. "3: Now as he was going along and approaching Damascus, suddenly a light from heaven flashed around him. 4: He fell to the ground and heard a voice saying to him, 'Saul, why do you persecute me?' 5: He asked, 'Who are you, Lord?' The reply came, 'I am Jesus, whom you are persecuting.'" Saul, as a theologian, believed in the Jewish laws. Nowhere in scripture have I read of a relationship between Jesus and Saul. While using my spiritual imagination, I would conclude that Saul was in school as a student under the leadership of the Pharisees counsel and the stories of the divine works of Jesus were discussed in class, and they denounced the acts of Jesus as blasphemy. This might be his reason for standing and watching with approval of the stoning of Stephen. Not a stone in hand, but watched in agreement of the action of those who remained under the law.

While on the road to Damascus, he was on a mission to bring them, which were there bound unto Jerusalem. The Light of the world blinded him for three days. After being led to the city of Damascus, Jesus spoke to a disciple named Ananias in a dream to get up and go to the streets and find a man of Tarsus in the home of Judas named Saul. "12: At this moment he is praying," and he has seen in a vision. A man named Ananias came in and laid hands on him so that he might regain his sight.

Ananias was selected from the congregation to lay hands on; today the hands would be used to point the new person in the right directions, to help the new person to select the food of life to strengthen his relationship with God. What a greater advantage to a person if his mentor is married and has children. His spiritual life would bloom into a flower of new life as he witnesses his family growing into the plans of God.

Paul and Ananias together preached that Jesus of Nazareth was the Jewish Messiah and the Son of God. Not only was he commissioned to preach to the Jews but also to the Romans and Gentiles of the world. So we conclude that the power of regeneration transforms a sinner into a meaningful saint when he or she allows the Holy Spirit to help in this transformation. With the help of the Holy Spirit and the leadership of the Church, a new person can reach their place of honor, a personal relationship with God as they grow from one paradigm of old into a paradigm of newness. Regeneration is part of the "Salvation packages." First a new birth. The new birth is a spiritual, holy, and heavenly birth signified by a being made alive in a spiritual sense. Our first birth was one of spiritual death because of the first sin. Man in his natural state is "dead in trespasses and sins" until we are made alive by Christ when we place our faith in him (Ephesians 2:1). After regeneration, we can see the wondrous works of our creator, and we hear in clarity the voice of the Holy Spirit as he guides us, and we develop a strong desire to seek after divine things, and to live a life of faith and holiness.

Jesus has taken up residence in our hearts; we become now partakers of the divine nature, having been made new creatures. Please remain mindful that God, not man, is the source of this (Ephesians 2:1, 8). Man has no works but by God's own loving will and pleasure. His great love and free gift, his rich and daily grace and abundant mercy, are the cause of it, and these attributes of God are displayed in the power of regeneration and conversion of sinners.

Its Motivation

The healing power of regenerations can be seen through the eyes of the re-generated being. The scares of the past have become a heavy burden, some so strong that its actions cause cancer, damaging the mind, body, and soul of the person. Only after the regeneration process will the healing process begin.

Baptismal regeneration is the belief that is necessary for salvation, or more precisely that regeneration does not occur until a person is water baptized. Advocates of baptismal regeneration point to Scripture verses such as Mark 16:16, John 3:5, Acts 2:38, Acts 22:16, Galatians 3:27, and 1 Peter 3: 21 for Biblical support. And, granted, those verses seem to indicate that baptism is necessary for salvation.

Advocates of baptismal regeneration typically have a four-part formula for how salvation is received. They believe that a person must believe, repent, confess, and be baptized in order to be saved because if you confess with your lips that Jesus is Lord and believe in your heart that God raised him from the dead, you will be saved. "10: For one believes with the heart and so is justified, and one confesses with the mouth and so is saved" (Romans 10:9-10).

"38: Peter said to them, 'Repent, and be baptized every one of you in the name of Jesus Christ so that your sins may be forgiven; and you will receive the gift of the Holy Spirit'" (Acts 2:38). Confession, understood Biblically, is a demonstration of faith. If a person has truly received Jesus Christ as Savior, proclaiming that faith to others will be a result. If a person is ashamed of Christ and is ashamed of the message of the Gospel, it is highly unlikely that the person has understood the Gospel or experienced the salvation that Christ provided. Repentance, understood Biblically, is required for salvation; repentance is a change of mind. Repentance, in relation to salvation, helps in a changed mind from rejection of Christ to acceptance of faith. One cannot receive Jesus Christ as Savior by grace through faith, without a change of mind about who He is and what He did.

Baptism, understood Biblically, is identification with Christ. Christian baptism illustrates a believer's identification with Christ's death, burial, and resurrection (Romans 6:3-4). As with confession, if a person is unwilling to be baptized and unwilling to identify his or her life as being redeemed by Jesus Christ, that person has very likely not been made a new creation (2 Corinthians 5:17) through faith in Jesus Christ. Dr. Evans' interpretation to the Epistle of St. Paul to the Romans addresses the scriptures of baptismal regeneration: "3: Know ye not, that so many of us as were baptized into Jesus Christ were baptized into death, 4: therefore we are buried with him by baptism into death: that like as Christ was raised up from the dead by thy glory of the Father, even so we also should walk in newness of life." In general, we are dead to sin, that is in profession and in obligation. Our baptism signifies our cutting off from the kingdom of sin. We profess to have no more to do with sin. We are dead to sin by a participation of virtue, power for the killing of it, and by whom it is killed. All this is in vain if we persist in sin; we contradict a profession, violate an obligation, and return that to which we were dead, like walking ghosts. He that is dead is freed from sin; that is, he that is dead to it is freed from rule and dominion of it, as the servant that is dead is freed from his master (Job. 3:19).

Dr. Evans questions the reality of the eligibility of people who are still bound to the sins of addiction, adultery, murder, pride, and other acts against God. Now shall we be such fools as to return to that slavery from which we are discharged? When we are delivered out of Egypt, shall we talk of going to it again? One defining question should be asked, not only should they address changes of addictive behavior but address changes in their environment, as well as the people, places, and those things that are triggers that produce negative behavior that will change our pathway to rightness while carrying that old wooden cross while following Jesus. Being baptized in the name of the Father, His Son Jesus Christ, and the Holy Spirit binds all saints together. We come to be apprentices to Christ as our teacher, and it is our allegiance to

Christ as our sovereign. We were baptized into his death, into a participation of the privileges purchased by his death, and into obligation both to comply with the design of his death, which was to redeem us from all iniquity, and to conform to the pattern of his death. That was the profession and promise of our baptism, and we do not do well if we do not answer this profession and make good this promise. Sanctification is the work of God's free grace, whereby we are renewed in the whole man, after the image of God, and are enabled more and more to die unto sin and live unto righteousness. Our creed concerning Jesus Christ is, among others things, that he was crucified, dead, and buried; now baptism is a sacramental conformity to him in each of these, as the Apostle here takes notice. First, our old man is crucified with him; second, we are dead with Christ. Death on the cross was slow and painful. Christ is obedient to death; when he died, we might say to die with him, as is our dying to sin, is an act of conformity both to the design and to the example of Christ dying for sin.

Perseverance and grace means that continuing still in the state of grace and habitual practice of godliness to the end (John 10:28). "28: And I give unto them eternal life, and they shall never perish neither shall any man pluck them out of my hands." Salvation, through repentance, confession, and baptism, will result in healing of the mind and heart.

What effect does the breath of regeneration have in our society today as we are surrounded with the presences of hunger, poverty, homelessness, and poor medical services for the young and elderly? We are witnessing an increase of children crossing into America from Mexico through our border because of high crime rates and high poverty rates, not to mention lack of jobs and housing. America, the land of the brave, where you can become something in life, there they can find hope. Those children are the cause of government discussions today, and many of them have been placed around the United States in states where they will have an opportunity to become citizens, receive an education, and a way of life that is above the poverty of their country. They are placed in zones within the city and placed in an urban environment that forces them to change in order to survive.

The breath of regeneration, the breath of God remains; God is a living God whose grace and mercies are bestowed on the just as well as the unjust, the adult as well as the young. Our mission and our goal is to carry the Word of God to them so the words of God can be heard, "the good news of our re-deemer, Jesus Christ."

In the article written by Alice Park, "Stressed in the City: How Urban Life May Change Your Brain," she finds living in the city stressful take out in comparison to its cultures, energy and convenience and yet a fine place to live. I am sure she is not the only person who lives in a city that feels the same way. She reports that when it comes to mental health, the urban lifestyle may not be such a good thing. City dwellers tend to be more stressed and have higher levels of mood disorders and psychotic illnesses such as schizophrenia than those living in rural or suburban areas. And now researchers say they have un-covered certain changes in brain activity that could potentially help explain why. An international study was conducted by the University of Heidelberg and the Douglas Mental Health University Institute at McGill University, who reported in the journal *Nature* that people who live or were raised in the cities show distinct differences in activity in certain brain regions than those who are not city dwellers. One, they show higher activation in the amygdale, the brain region that regulates emotions such as anxiety and fear. Nine-Eleven in New York brought about emotional reactions to a heightened level as we who lived outside the city witnessed an increase of persons attending church serv-ices at a rate that matched the storm of Katharine in 2011. Poverty also plays a role in the increasing level of anxiety and fear. The Latest Census Reveals: 2012 poverty rate was 10.8 percent versus the 2013 poverty rate of 11.4 per-cent. The number of people living in poverty in 2012 was 934,943 versus 998,549 people living in poverty in 2013.

Mr. Melville D. Miller, president of the Legal Services of New Jersey, said the increase could be attributed to the fact that even those previously unem-ployed who have found work may still not be earning enough to raise above the poverty level. By county the highest rate is found in Cumberland County, and the lesser is found in Hunterdon County. As we witness an increase of God's children crossing the border of Mexico and those coming in through Canada, they are being placed in our cities.

The breath of regeneration, the Word of God, is readily available for all of his children, pastors, and the church leaders who are commissioned to go and preach the Gospel to the entire world. In this case, the world is now mi-grating to America. And when we fail to share the Gospel, we become disobedient. We are to approach our brothers and sister with a pure heart and a living spirit. Not only are we to reach out to those living in the city but also to those who live in the country. The country for a city dweller is truly a different paradigm. Mr. Thomas Sprawling, author of *City Life versus Country Life*, finds the country life a much more pleasing lifestyle compared to the stress of city life. I can remember when I was a young child lying on my grandmother's living room floor and asking my grandmother about the unlocked door. She, without even looking up from her sewing, answered that there was no one out there that would be bothering us. It was far different than anything I had ever witnessed before. Even the unlocked door still may remain true in some southern cities; crimes and drugs have reached the country at a high rate. One of every ten black males or females have engaged in some type of drug usage from age thirteen to fifty and faced some type of legal problems. The missionary role has not stopped because more people are returning back to the South.

Today more than one hundred fifty million people live in a country they were not born in. About thirteen million of those are refugees; the rest voluntarily left their homeland to seek a better life. As *The Economist* reported, the Census Bureau forecasted that by 2050 "the Hispanic population will have increased by 200 percent, the population as a whole by 50 percent, and whites, only 30 percent." Once again the immigration policy is now the hot national topic. Today more Mexicans live in Los Angeles than in any city in Mexico, with the exception of Mexico City and Guadalajara. More Cambodians live in Long Beach, California, than in Phnom Penh, Cambodia. More Filipinos are living in the Hmong capital of the world outside of Laos, and central California is the center of Sikh life in the United States. According to the recent Urban Institute report, 22 percent of all U.S. children younger than six have immigrant parents.

Peter's visit to Antioch was to sit with Paul and Barnabas and the church congregation. At first Peter demonstrated that agape love he had witnessed and learned from our Lord Jesus Christ. But as a certain Jewish representative of the Jerusalem church also came to visit, Peter stopped eating with his new Gentile friends (Gal 2:12). The Bible reports that Peter was afraid of those leaders, maybe because of his concerns of what they might think about him, or because of the fact that they were non-Jewish believers.

When Paul observed his behavior, he questioned his action. He felt that with Peter's withdrawal it made the new Gentiles feel as if they were second-class citizens. This poisoned behavior was seen in Peter by other leaders in attendance. Paul handled himself in a manner as outlined in The New National Baptist Hymnal "Church Covenant." In case of differences of opinion in the Church, we will strive to avoid a contentious spirit, and if we cannot unanimously agree we will cheerfully recognize the right of the majority to govern.

Of course, Paul confronted Peter in public, in front of all of the believers (Gal 2:11-14). Peter thought differently after his encounter with Paul; it was evident by the fact that he continued to work and demonstrate concern for the Gentiles (1 Peter 2:12) and developed a deep respect for Paul, whom he called his beloved brother, and acknowledged his writing as being with wisdom (2 Pet 3:15).

The breath of regeneration as seen through the eyes of Paul while on his missionary mission in Antioch has to be a moment of great pleasure to witness firsthand, the mighty works of God's sovereignty of his grace. God has called thousands to join in a personal relationship with him. According to the Bible, the Lord "calls" or summons people to do certain things. In a general sense, God calls all men to receive the salvation and the redemption that can be found only in his son Jesus Christ (Rom. 8:30, 1 Cor. 1:9, 1 Thes. 2:12).

In Timothy Morton's book, "Called Into the Ministry," God calls and commands all men everywhere to repent and receive Christ. Though this calling is for all men, it is a call to the individual. God personally and individually invites and commands each individual to partake of the blessings of His redemption. This call is given outwardly by the Gospel (2 Thes. 2:14) and inwardly by the Holy Spirit (Rev. 22:17). Those who refuse God's gracious call will be eternally held accountable for their refusal (John 12:48).

This calling is more than just an invitation, though; it is a command (Acts 17:30). Paul was not refrained from visiting those places considered unclean under the law. His mission was clear; go forth and preach the Gospel to all nations, baptize in the name of the Father, Son, and Holy Spirit. The fresh air of the Lord was present in Antioch. His words brought new spiritual life, and the light of Jesus shined on a nation of Gentiles. This sovereign work of God in regeneration was also predicted in the prophecy of Ezekiel. Through him God promised a time in the future when he would give new spiritual life to his people: "A new heart also will I give you, and a new spirit will I put within you: and I will take away the stony heart out of your flesh, and I will give you a heart of flesh. And I will put my spirit within you, and cause you to walk in my statutes, and ye shall keep my judgments, and do them" (Ezek. 36:26, 27, KJV).

Jesus' Breath on His Apostles

Found in the book of (John 20: 19-22), then the same day at evening, being the first day of the week, when the doors were shut where the disciples were assembled for fear of the Jews, came Jesus, who stood in the midst and said unto them, "Peace be unto you." And when he had so said, he showed unto them his hands and his side. Then were the disciples glad, when they saw the Lord. Then said Jesus to them again, "Peace be unto you: as my Father hath sent me, even so send I you." And when he had said this, he breathed on them and said unto them, "Receive ye the Holy Spirit."

When Jesus breathed on his disciples, he UN-locked the shut door; the fear of the Jewish leaders was not a factor any longer. We have felt and witnessed the Holy Spirit at work once inside our heart. The regeneration power of God produces a slow but rewarding change; the fearless become meek, the meek become stronger, those who are last become first. For Adam and Eve, they lost the Holy Spirit that was breathed into them by the Father during their creation.

Even before His death and resurrection, Jesus called all of his disciples together and selected twelve from the many who followed. The twelve were ordained and titled Apostle; they were commission by Jesus to go out and preach "the kingdom of heaven is at hand." "1: And when he had called unto him his twelve disciples, he gave them power against unclean spirits, to cast them out, and to heal all manner of sickness and all manner of disease" (Mat. 10:1).

The word "Apostle" comes from the Greek word "apostello," which means "to send forth with a commission." It was used by the Greeks for the personal representative of the king, ambassadors who functioned with the king's authority. Today job descriptions for leaders have changed based on the faith base of the individual: bishop, Apostle, pastor, deacon, deaconess, teacher, and preacher. All have spiritual job descriptions as outlined in 1 Timothy 3:1-13. A bishop must be blameless, the husband of one wife, vigilant, sober, of good behavior, given to hospitality, apt to teach, not given to wine, no striker, not greedy of filthy lucre but patient, not a brawler, not covetous, one that ruleth well his own house, having his children in subjection with all gravity, not a novice, lest being lifted up with pride he fall into the condemnation of the devil. Moreover, he must have a good report of them who are without, lest he fall into reproach and the snare of the devil. These qualifications of a bishop are closely applied to the deacons and teachers' positions.

A man had to meet certain qualifications to be an Apostle of Jesus Christ. He must have seen the risen Christ (1 Cor. 9:1) and fellowshipped with Him (Acts 1:21-22). He had to be chosen by the Lord (Eph. 4:11). The Apostle laid the foundation of the Church (Eph. 2:20) and then passed from the scene. While all believers are sent forth to represent the King (John 17:18; 20:21), no believer today can claim to be an Apostle, for none of us have seen the risen Christ (1 Peter 1:8).

The power that was given to the disciples (Apostle) was not identified as being the breath of Jesus being blown on them, or was it divinely placed on them by His touch, or it could have been presented to them through words. If He introduced it through sermon, He still used the gift of breath to produce its creation. In the book of Genesis, God created heaven and earth with just the spoken words "Let it be," and it was so. The secret of power. One cannot receive it until it is given and one will not have to "take it by faith" after it is given. The work of salvation could be accomplished only by Jesus Christ, and He did it alone. But the witness of this salvation could only be accomplished by His people, those who have trusted Him and have been saved. The King needed ambassadors to carry the message, and He still needs them. "Whom shall I send and who will go for us? (Isa. 6:8). Before Jesus sent His ambassadors out to minister, He preached an "ordination sermon" to encourage and prepare them.

The breath of Jesus in likeness of God the Father delivered unto them the Holy Spirit, the third God of the Trinity. The regeneration power that was given to the Apostles was as the breath into the nostrils of Adam and Eve. Jesus in His sermon inhaled and exhaled, forming words of encouragement. I can envision our Lord placing His hands upon each one's head as they readied themselves for their mission of sharing the Gospel message of salvation.

Christ's commission given to the twelve Apostles is not our commission today. He sent them only to the people of Israel to the Jewish people first, which is a historical pattern because the salvation of the Jews. The twelve ambassadors while traveling were proclaiming the coming of the kingdom just as John the Baptist had done. Our message today is "Christ died for our sins" and not "The Kingdom of heaven is at hand." The King has come; He has already suffered, died, and risen from the dead. He offers His salvation to all who will believe.

LIFE IN THE GARDEN OF EDEN

Once again using my spiritual imagination, I can see living in the Garden of Eden, which could be reminiscent of living in the coming heaven. The final heaven as described in the book of Revelation is where the Lamb of God will call His residents home to reside for eternity. Heaven (home), where God Himself will wipe away the tears from the eyes, will proclaim there shall be no more death, neither sorrow, nor crying, neither shall there be any more pain for the former things are passed away. "21: And there came unto me one of the seven angels which had the seven vials full of the seven last plagues, and talked with me, saying, Come hither, I will show thee the bride, the Lamb's wife. And he carried me away in the spirit to a great and high mountain, and showed me that great city, the holy Jerusalem, descending out of heaven from God, Having the glory of God: and her light was like unto a stone most precious, even like a jasper stone, clear as crystal; and had a wall great and high, and had twelve gates, and at the gates twelve angels, and names written thereon, which are the names of the twelve tribes of the children of Israel: On the east three gates; on the north three gates; and in them the names of the twelve Apostles of the Lamb. And he that talked with me had a golden reed to measure the city, and the gates thereof, and the wall thereof. And the city lieth foursquare, and the length is as large as the breadth: and he measured the city with the reed, twelve thousand furlongs. The length and the breadth and the height of it are equal. And he measured the wall thereof, an hundred and forty and four cubits, according to the measure of a man, that is, of the angel. And the building of the wall of it was of jasper: and the city was pure gold, like unto clear glass. And the foundations of the wall of the city were garnished with all manner of precious stones. The first foundation was jasper; the second, sapphire; the third, a chalcedony; the fourth, an emerald; the fifth, sardonyx; the sixth, sardius; the seventh, chrysopras; the eleventh, a jacinth; the twelfth, an amethyst. And the twelve gates were adored with twelve pearls; and the street of the city was pure gold, as it was transparent glass. And I saw no temple therein: for the Lord God Almighty and the Lamb are the temples of it. And the city had no need of the sun, neither of the moon to shine in it: for the glory of God did lighten it, and the Lamb is the light thereof. And the nations of them which are saved shall walk in the light of it: and the kings of the earth do bring their glory and honor into it. And the gates of it shall not be shut at all by day: for there shall be no night there. And they shall bring the glory and honour of the nations into it. And there shall in no wise enter into it anything that defileth, neither whatsoever worketh abomination, nor maketh a lie: but they which are written in the Lamb's book of life."

Our Lord and Savior Jesus Christ, before his death, resurrection, and his ascension into heaven, explained to his disciples: "Let not your heart be troubled: ye believe in God, believe also in me. In my Father's house are many mansions: if it were not so, I would have told you. I go to prepare a place for you. And if I go and prepare a place for you, I will come again, and receive you unto myself; that where I am, there ye may be also" (John 14:1-3). Jesus informs the disciples that heaven is where the loving Apostles will reside in the New Jerusalem with Him in all of its glory. In the cosmic theory of the ancient world, and of the Hebrews in particular, the earth was flat, lying between a great pit into which the shadows of the dead departed, and the heaven above in which God and the angels dwelt, and it came to be thought that it was where the righteous dwelled after having been raised from the dead to live forever. It was natural to think of heaven as concave above the earth and resting on some foundation, possibly of pillars, set at the extreme horizon.

The Hebrews, like other ancient people, believed in a plurality of heavens, and the literature of Judaism speaks of seven. In the highest, or Aravoth, was the throne of God. Although the descriptions of these heavens varied, it would seem that it was not unusual to regard the third heaven as paradise. It was to this that Paul said he had been caught up. This series of superimposed heaven was regarded as filled by different sorts of superhuman beings. The second heaven in later Jewish thought was regarded as the abode of evil spirits and angels awaiting punishment. The New Testament, however, does not commit itself to these precise speculations, although in Eph. 6:12 it speaks of spiritual host of wickedness who dwell in heavenly places. This conception of heaven as being above a flat earth underlies many religious expressions that are still current. There have been various attempts to locate heaven, as for example, in Sirius as the central sun of our system. Similarly, there have been innumerable speculations, however, that lie outside the region of positive knowledge and rest ultimately on the cosmogony of prescientific times. They may be of value in cultivating religious emotion, but they belong to the region of speculation. The Biblical descriptions of heaven are not scientific, but symbolical. Practically all these are to be found in the Johannine Apocalypse. It was undoubtedly conceived eschatologically by the New Testament writers, but they maintained a great reserve in all of their descriptions of the life of the redeemed. It is, however, possible to state definitely that while they conceived of the heavenly condition as involving social relations, they did not regard it as one in which the physical organism survived. The sensuous descriptions of heaven to be found in the Jewish apocalypses and in Mohammedanism are altogether excluded by the sayings of Jesus relative to marriage in the new age and those of Paul relative to the "spiritual body." The prevailing tendency at the present time among theologians, to regard heaven as a state of the soul rather than a place, belongs likewise to the region of opinion. The degree of probability will be determined by one's general view as to the nature of immortality. Dr. Mathews could have concluded by stating that the individual who is in favor with Christ will "see for himself." Praises be to our Lord and Savior because I also will be obtaining a new residence in heaven with him.

The life in the Garden of Eden was perfect, and if Adam and Eve had obeyed God and not eaten the fruit of the forbidden tree they could have lived there for eternity. But after disobeying, Adam and Eve no longer deserved residences in paradise, and God's final judgment was eviction.

If they had continued to live in the Garden of Eden and not eaten from the tree of life, they would have lived forever. But eternal life in a state of sin would mean forever trying to hide from God. The Garden of Eden is described by the book of Genesis as being the place where the first man and woman were created by God and lived until they fell and were expelled. In the Qur'an it is simply called the Garden. It places no divine beauty in its sight; a Garden can be depicted as a plot of soil that will produce fruits, vegetables, and flowers, which also have to be tended and cultivated. The commonness between the two is the oneness they have with God. God, the creator of heaven and earth, planted the seeds, which without care will grow to cover the earth with natural beauty throughout all seasons.

The origin of the term "Eden," which is Hebrew means "delight," may be related to the Akkadian Edina, which derives from the Sumerian EDIN. The latter word means "plan." The Garden of Eden is also described as a paradise where the first family lived naked and not ashamed among the animals and a great variety of fruit-bearing trees. They could freely eat of the fruit of all the trees except one that God prohibited them from eating, called the tree of the Knowledge of Good and Evil. Satan is symbolized by a serpent tempting them to eat of the forbidden fruit, and as a result humanity was expelled from the Garden of Eden, to never return.

In today's society, our Garden of Eden is not a place of paradise for some of God's children. So many people find themselves living in low-economy housing (the ghetto), which is infested with diseases, roaches, and rats, a place unsuitable for any human to live. It becomes a place out of the elements that they call home and place to raise their children, a place where they can pray and call on God to help them as they go through the many storms of life. It's Paradise, but if evicted they would have to be placed in a homeless shelter. For the homeless, the sun, moon, and stars are their place of residence. A child who runs away from their home finds paradise in a homeless shelter or a jail cell in a correctional facility.

There are many stories told about how those living in such conditions are delivered. Their story includes a special relationship with Jesus as he becomes their strong tower to run into during the mean storms. Worshiping God during Chaplin services brought them closer and closer to experience His love. They tell of their stories of the Spirit of lacking entering into their homes, affecting their finances and food shortages. All prayers are reaching the listening ears of God, who is always on time. At all times we are to continue to praise God, in bad times and good times aplenty. Our paradise is in our relationship with God.

The location of Eden is the subject of much speculation. The Genesis account describes Eden as located at the junction of four major rivers, two of which exist today: the Tigris and the Euphrates. Some scholars predict it's located in the Persian Gulf; others seek a location somewhere in Africa, where the first humans are said to have appeared. Many believe that Eden was not an actual physical location but a state of blessed existence that was lost when Adam and Eve fell and lost their oneness with God.

The Garden of Eden is recognized in Abrahamic religions of Judaism, Christianity, and Islam. Some other religions and cultures have a creation story containing a similar concept to the Biblical Garden of Eden, ascribing various locations to place of first habitation.

From the beginning, God's relationship to people has been based on giving first; he gave us life. Humanity was not only formed by God but was also created in God's very image and care, like that of a potter molding clay. God gave humanity the breath of life. The other living creatures also received the breath of life from God, but God's creation of Adam and Eve was different. God gave only to people the unique quality of being created in the divine image. We were given the ability to have a deep, abiding relationship with the Creator. God continues to give as He blesses human beings with authority over the rest of the earthly creation.

Humans were given the plants to use for food and a home in the Garden of Eden, for Eden was a place where all physical needs would have been met.

Dr. Allen asks in his book titled *Basic Studies in Soteriology*, how did this fall of Adam and Eve leave them spiritually? After being banned from the Garden of Eden, both Adam and Eve became spiritually dead; the verdict of guilty was announced, and the spiritual element in them was withdrawn from them. The one and only element that gave them communication with God had been taken; their close relationship with Him was no longer available. Adam, the creation of God, formed out of the dust of the earth, could no longer inhale the breath of God as he sat in dialogue with him in the coolness of the day. As the divine spirit of God continually shined in and out of him, which Eve adorned was no longer present.

Mankind now at birth is born in sin. This act of disobedience cursed all. There is no living divine Holy Spirit element in us, and that is the very element that we need if we are to be able to understand anything of a divine nature.

We cannot even want to believe in God; we do not even want to be obedient to God in a true sense. We may be willing to follow a god but not the God of the Bible, but only the many other gods that people worship in our world today. Even those who do claim to worship Him do not worship in the ways outlined in the Bible any more than those who do not even know the existence of God.

God's Love Clothed Them

Unto Adam and his wife, the Lord God, who loved them, made them clothes made out of animal skin before their evictions. Yes, God, who created both Adam and Eve, had to discipline them, but His love for them was unchanging. The first blood was shed by God, who selected the animals to give up their life so that His creation would be clothed. Nothing is too hard for God; the selection of the animal, death, and disrobing them of their skin can be accomplished within seconds, which would cause no pain for the animal. But for man, the process would have taken a bit longer and would have been somewhat of an ordeal. First, you would have to select an animal whose skin is without blemish and shows a healthy disposition. The second step would be to separate them from the other herd. At the same time, you would have to find a location large enough to work.

I have learned that once the animal has been selected and in your work area, you must render the animal unconscious by applying an electric shock or a bolt pistol to the front of the animal's head. The animal then should be hung upside down and his artery and jugular vein severed with a knife. The head is removed, and after the front and rear feet are removed the hind skin is removed by a downward pulling on the skin.

My assumption is that God called the animals and commanded them to give up their lives, and their skin was removed. I can imagine God would not leave the carcass lying on the ground to rot; this was of course the Garden of Eden (Paradise). Everything was in place and in working order for the good.

God speaks to the earth, and a rocky mound appears and the carcass placed on top of the rock and God called for fire to consume it. Can you imagine Adam and Eve, who covered themselves with leaves, watching all that God was doing? Adam was learning while watching God as the aroma of the animal fat was consumed as it entered into the air. Adam saw God's response as a pleasing moment; there was hope and possibly a chance for repentance from God that could be obtained, a form of regeneration, a hint of renewal with God can be. Eve learned as well; she observed the use of the animal, which her husband labored to name.

The fire produced a pleasing order, and within seconds the meat was consumed by fire. This was the fire offering unto God; Adam and Eve were clothed and banished from the Garden of Eden.

Dr. Allen suggests that spiritual death was afforded Adam and Eve after their fall, being banned from the Garden. They were unable to have a face-to-face communication with God. Outside the Garden, Adam and Eve were faced with the problems of shelter, food, and fire. Inside the Garden, they never had to concern themselves with those physical needs because God's divine glory provided all that was needed. God gave them instructions on what to eat and what not to eat. And out of the ground made the Lord God to grow every tree that is pleasant to the sight, and good for food; the tree of life also in the midst of the Garden, and the tree of the knowledge of good and evil (Gen. 2:9).

The name of the tree of the knowledge of good and evil implies that evil had already occurred, if not in the Garden, then at the time of Satan's fall from heaven. Not only is Eve able to have dialogue with God but also Satan, who has taken on the form of a serpent that is described as "craftier than any of the wild animals the Lord God had made." The serpent introduced a question to Eve about eating of the fruit in the Garden, especially the tree of knowledge, which God announced as being "off limits." "'Surely you will not die,' proclaimed the serpent, 'for God knows that when you eat from it your eyes will be opened, and you will be like God, knowing good and evil.'"

Satan used a sincere motive to tempt Eve: "You will become just like God." It wasn't wrong of Eve to want to be like God. To become more like God is humanity's highest goal; it's what we are supposed to pursue in our relationship with Him, to get closer, to seek His face. But Satan misled Eve concerning the right way to accomplish this goal. He told her that she could become more like God by defying God's authority, by taking God's place and deciding for herself what was best for her in life. In effect, he told her to become her own god.

My understanding is that "once Adam and Eve had taken their first bite of the forbidden fruit, disobedience, murder, and sin was already committed; inside their minds and spiritual body a transformation had taken place." God, who is all knowing, felt the loss of power and began to look for his children, and then the man and his wife heard the sound of God walking in the Garden in the cool of the day, and they hid themselves among the trees of the Garden. But the Lord called to them, "Where are you?"

The sin had been committed; the Judge is sited as the prosecutor; the Word of God is cross-examining them, asking questions of their whereabouts and what brought them to their awareness of their nakedness. The jury, consisting of the third person of the Trinity, the Holy Spirit, is waiting to be dismissed for deliberation. Their eyes were open, shame overcame them, the need to hide themselves empowered them, and to cover themselves as the spirit of fear became a new experience.

God is concerned that you and I understand the seriousness of sin and the reality of spiritual death. The series of events included provides an unmistakable demonstration of the death principle operating in human experience. We see death in the sudden flash of shame that spread over Adam and Eve as they recognized their nakedness. Today the more "mature" defend public nakedness as morally natural. "Evil is in the eye of the beholder" is the phrase they often use to attack anyone who objects, never realizing how condemning that excuse is. Evil is in the eye of the beholder, not in the creation of God. But since the fall, the eye is evil! We see death demonstrated in the first pair's flight from God. They had known His love, yet awareness of guilt alienated them from Him and they tried to hide. We see death in Adam's refusal to accept responsibility for his choice. He tried to shift the blame, first to Eve and then ultimately to God Himself. "It was the woman you gave me who brought me some" (Genesis 3:12).

We find hope in God's actions as He clothed the naked pair in animal skins, the first indication that for redemption blood must be shed. The first blood speaks of sacrifice, and sacrifice speaks of Christ.

We find hope in God's action in seeking out the sinning couple. Sin will distort our idea of God, erecting a grim barrier that we are unwilling to approach. But God came into the Garden seeking Adam, just as later Jesus came into the world to seek and to save those who were lost.

The law of influence: Eve, the negative influence; regardless of their titles, real leaders influence others. The story of Eve demonstrates the impact of negative influence. Although God commissioned Adam as her spiritual leader, Eve usurped the role of influencer. Adam followed his wife rather than God, and together they led humankind into sin.

Adam, the first leader to drop the ball; at the moment he received God's mandate to rule the earth, Adam became the first spiritual leader in human history. Initially, this meant overseeing the Garden and providing direction to his family. Adam was to be a good steward over his resources and relationships. Unfortunately, he failed on both counts.

When Eve brought the forbidden fruit to Adam, he mismanaged God's creation by eating it. Adam also mismanaged his wife by remaining passive when he should have taken a stand, thus allowing both Eve and himself to fall morally.

Spiritual leadership isn't complex; it simply requires a willingness to take responsibility. Sadly, many spiritual leaders continue to duplicate Adam's mistake by shirking their responsibilities at home, in the neighborhood, on the job, and in the Church. They forget that while Adam's failure started at home, in just a short time it damaged all who would come after him; his disobedience spoiled the beauty of the Garden, his place of residence where he and his wife lived and ultimately devastated the entire world. And the whole mess can be traced back to one spineless refusal to lead.

Life outside the Garden of Eden

The definition of the word "life" is the sequence and mental experiences that make up the existence of an individual. The Greek word "bias," meaning "life," its English derivative means "antibiotic," "autobiography," "biography," "biology," "biopsy," and "bios." The Hebrew meaning is from the toast "I" chayim, meaning "to life."

Self-originated movement, especially as seen in locomotion and breathing, were naturally the earliest criteria of life. Scientists investigate life as merely a mode of motion. Life, however, has not yet yielded its secrets to human inquiry; not yet has life, by any experiment, been produced from purely inorganic origins.

We theistic remain faithful to the view of creation, which holds an entirely worthy and satisfactory position in following the creation narratives as written in the book of Genesis. To God is all the glory for life, to God, who gives to all life and breath and in all things.

The life of Adam and Eve, as we have already discussed, was a divine act of God, forming the dust of the earth and shaping it into a shape of a man, breathing into him his breath, which produced life. Our creator with love created from the rib of man a helpmate, who was named by man as woman; her birth given name was Eve. She also was given life by the means of the breath of God.

Outside life, we find Adam and Eve no longer in the presence of God but the presence of God was with them; they were unable to sit face to face and have an enriching conversation with him. They were distanced from His presence by their disobediences, due to the mismanagement of Adam and weakness of Eve to be influenced by a desire to be like God. While distant from God, they were unable, and without, a personal connecting relationship with Him; they no longer were able to walk with him in the coolness of the day. Adam and Eve were unable to receive his purity breath, which contains His regeneration power.

Now Adam and Eve were faced with the social problem of finding shelter (housing), obtaining food (grocery shopping), health, and insurance policies, and most importantly the atonement spirit in reestablishing a relationship with God. The hope, which also banished with them, became a common thought and a daily phrase interjected into Adam's prayer life. In the contradiction between the word of promise and the experiential reality of suffering and death. Faith takes its stand on hope and "hastens beyond this world."

Calvin did not mean by this statement that Christian faith flees the world, but he did mean it crosses and transcends boundaries, to be engaged in an exodus. Yet this happens in a way that does not suppress or skip the unpleasant realities of life. Death is real, and decay is putrefying decay. Guilt remains guilt and suffering remains, even for the believer, a cry to which there is no ready-made answers. Faith does not overstep these realities into a heavenly utopia or a place of paradise.

It can overlap the bounds of life, with their closed walls of suffering, guilt, and death, only at the point where they have in actual fact been broken through. It is only in following the risen Christ, who was raised from suffering, from a God-forsaken death and from the grave that it gains an open prospect in which there is nothing more to oppress us, a view of the realm of freedom and of joy. Faith recognizes the dawning of this future of openness and freedom in the Christ. Hope is therefore the inseparable companion of faith. When this hope is taken away, however eloquently or elegantly, we discourse concerning faith; we are convicted of having none. Hope is nothing else than the expectation of those things that faith has believed to have been truly promised by God. The modern idea of hope is "to wish for, to expect, but without certainty of the fulfillment, to desire much, but with no real assurances of getting your desire."

Adam's assurance of hope is in the hands of the Judge, who sits in on the highest court of the land, the one who created not only him and his family but the heavens and the earth. This same hope carried by Adam is the same hope we carry daily in our prayer life each morning as we drop to our knees.

For we were saved in his hope, but hope that is seen is not hope, for why does one still hope for what he sees? But if we hope for what we do not see, we eagerly wait for it with perseverance. Likewise, the Spirit also helps in our weaknesses. For we do not know what we should pray for as we ought, but the Spirit Himself makes intercession for us with groaning that which cannot be uttered. Now He who searches the heart knows what the mind of the Spirit is because He makes intercession for the saints according to the will of God.

In the Christian life, faith has the priority but hopes the primacy. Without faith's knowledge of Christ, hope becomes a utopia and remains hanging in the air. But without hope, faith falls to pieces, becoming a fainthearted and ultimately a dead faith. It is through faith that man finds the path of true life, but it is only hope that keeps him on the pathways of life. It is that faith in Christ that gives hope its assurance. It is hope that gives faith in Christ, its breadth, and leads it into life.

Adam, while in his storm of life, used the spirit of hope in his prayers and, with the help of the Holy Spirit of God acting as an intercessor, helped his request to reach the ears of God.

Genesis 4:1: "Adam slept with his wife and she became pregnant, when the time had come she gave birth through the curse of pain to her first child and named him Cain. She gave praise unto God. 'With the Lord's help, I have brought forth a man!'" While in the presence of God in the Garden of Eden, Adam and Eve did not experience problems with pain or aging as they continued to work through their sentence imposed by God. Outside, Adam still lived a long life, and now he had become a father.

Eve's statement of "with God's help" she did press through the pain. His love covered them and now our God, who performed the first surgery to remove a rib from man, His second surgery was to remove the skin of his loving and obedient sheep to cover their nakedness, and now we find God in the delivery room as a doctor, a midwife, and a nurse. Was there still a relationship with God, a form of communication between Adam and God? Envision Adam and Eve with Baby Cain in their arms while kneeling, facing the direction of the Garden of Eden, and near him there was a burnt offering from a chosen lamb, and its fat was engulfed in flames as the smoke filled the air as a pleasing aroma reached God and as they were praising God for all that he had done.

The alter built was his first and not his last, as Adam would continue to attempt to strengthen his relationship with God, a sacrifice of the finest sheep, and its fat; the first fruits of their labor were presented unto Him.

The first family again was blessed by God to give birth to a second son, whom they named Abel. How pleasing it was for the family as they performed another alter sacrifice of thanksgiving unto God.

No longer was everything provided for Adam and Eve as it was in the Garden of Eden, where their daily task was refreshing and delightful. Now they had to struggle against the elements in order to provide food, clothing, and shelter for themselves and with two additions to the family. His sons learned to be faithful to their parents and in doing so learned who God was and to recognize his voice. Cain became a farmer working with the soil, and Able became a shepherd tending to the loving, obedient sheep.

His name in the Greek testament is spelled "Kain" while in the Hebrew text the name Cain has a different meaning (qyn), meaning "spear," coming from the root word "cluster." But it is clear that the narrative was at one time independent of Adam and Eve; it presupposes a much later stage in human progress. The distinction between pastoral and agricultural life, and between fruit and animal offering, the custom of blood revenge, and the large increase in the number of humans, from the first creation, indirect Cain's fear of being slain, in his processional of a wife and in his erection of a city, all show that a long period must be understood to have elapsed since the primitive condition of the first created couple.

Cain, the eldest of the brothers, as written becomes a farmer of the earth, the earth which was cursed by God. "65: And to Adam He said, 'Because you have listened and given heed to the voice of your wife and have eaten of the tree of which I commanded you, saying, You shall not eat of it, the ground is under a curse because of you; in sorrow and toil shall you eat (of the fruits) of it all the days of your life.'" God's curse of the ground would set in motion the stage that caused the first death of Abel, Cain's brother.

And in the process of time, it came to pass that Cain brought as his first offering unto the Lord fruit from the curse ground. And Abel, he also brought of the firstlings of his flock and of the fat thereof. And the Lord had respect unto Abel and to the offering, but unto Cain and to his offering he had no respect.

Abel the shepherd, The Hebrew form (Hebhel) denotes "vapor or breath." Abel was a son of Adam and Eve and brother of Cain. But the narrative presupposes a long period had elapsed in human history since the primitive condition of the first pair. The difference between pastoral and agricultural life has come to be recognized, for Abel was a keeper of sheep, but Cain was a tiller of the ground. Nothing is said in the book of Genesis of the moral character or of the reason why his offering was more excellent than Cain's in the eyes of God. In Hebrew 12:24, the blood of sprinkling that speaketh better things that of Abel, in the latter cried for vengeance.

In Matthew 23:35 and Luke 11:51, Abel is named as the first of the true martyrs whose blood had been shed during the period covered by the Old Testament; the last was Zachariah.

Abel's offering was more pleasing to God because his was not a curse of the earth, which was cursed by God for the acts of disobediences of Adam and Eve. Sometimes we as God's children, while under the stripes and blood of our Lord and Savior Jesus Christ, find ourselves in the same state when it comes to our tithes and offering. We have full knowledge of our requirements but find ourselves short in our giving. This act of disobediences was also reported in the New Testament as a certain man named Ananias, also with his wife, Sapphira, sold a possession, and they kept back part of the proceeds, and he brought a certain part and laid it at the Apostle's feet. In the book of Acts 5:3, Peter said to him, "Ananias, why has Satan filled your heart to lie to the Holy Spirit and keep back part of the price of the land for yourself? While it remained, was it not your own? And after it was sold, was it not in your own control? Why have you conceived this thing in your heart? You have not lied to men but to God." Then Ananias, hearing these words, fell down and breathed his last.

It's recorded that within three hours his wife came in, not knowing what had happened to her husband, and she was asked the same from Peter and the ending results was the same: death.

For Cain, he was not subjected under the Holy Spirit as of the Apostle and other Jews of that era.

Pride, jealousy, and hatred filled his heart, and his thoughts affected his actions even after the good counsel from God.

Cain was very wroth, and his countenance fell. And the Lord said unto Cain, "Why art thou wroth? And why is thy countenance fallen? If thou doest well, shall thou not be accepted? And if thou does not well, sin lie at the door." In bringing the offering he did, Cain denied that he was a sinful creature under the sentence of divine condemnation. He insisted on approaching God's way. He offered to God the fruits of the ground, which God had cursed. He presented the product of his own toil, the work of his own hands, and God refused to receive it.

And unto thee shall be his desire, and thou shall rule over him. And Cain talked with Abel, his brother, and it came to pass that when they were in the field, Cain rose up against Abel, his brother, and slew him.

And the Lord said unto Cain, "Where is Abel, thy brother?" And he said, "I know not; am I my brother's keeper?" And he said, "What hast thou done? The voice of thy brother's blood cried unto me from the ground. And now art thou cursed from the earth, which hath opened her mouth to receive thy brother's blood from thy hand; when thou tillest the ground, it shall not henceforth yield unto thee her strength; a fugitive and a vagabond shall thou be in the earth." And Cain said unto the Lord, "My punishment is greater than I can bear. Behold, thou hast driven me out this day from the face of the earth; and from thy face shall I be hid; and I shall be a fugitive and a vagabond in the earth; and it shall come to pass, that every one that findeth me shall slay me."

And the Lord said unto him, "Therefore whosoever slayeth Cain, vengeance shall be taken on him sevenfold." And the Lord set a mark upon Cain, lest any finding him should kill him. And Cain went out from the presence of the Lord, and dwelt in the land of Nod, on the east of Eden" (Genesis 4:2-16).

In the Garden of Eden, God called for Adam and Eve and asked, "Where you are?" In likeness God was asking Cain, "Where is your brother, Abel? What have you done?" God cursed the ground for the first time while all was under the management of Adam: "You shall not eat of it; the ground is under a curse because of you; in sorrow and toil shall you eat of the fruits of it all the days of your life" (Genesis 3:17). The second curse is recorded as: "and now art thou cursed from the earth, which hath opened her mouth to receive thy brother's blood from thy hands. When you till the ground, it shall no longer yield to you its strength."

The life outside the Garden for Adam and Eve can be seen as explorers traveling into remote lands. With them God's grace travels, his love for them remains with them. Their decisions and actions as the family has placed many generational curses on mankind, some of which we are still under. But by the saving grace of God, we as his children still have the opportunity to be redeemed by the strips and bloodshed from the Lamb of God, Jesus Christ.

God's love for his creations remained even after Cain's action. Being banished and with the loss of communication from the presence of God was more than what Cain could bear. Unto Adam and Eve another son was given, Seth, and from Cain a son was given, Enoch.

GOD'S BREATH IS THE DIVINE TRUTH

Found in the article "Breath Is a Divine Truth," the author's opening is a poem.

> Breath is rhythm, the life rhythm of every living cell
> Breath is an activity, the rhythmic activity of every living cell
> Breath is a force behind every living cell.
> Breath is a truth, the divine truth in every living cell.

Deep breathing is a therapy in which the breath of life is accentuated. From a theological point of view, we see that our breath is the breath of life as we receive it from God. The origin of the word "breathed" as we read in Genesis 2:7 is found in the Hebrew word "Neshamah," which means "Breath of God," "Spirit of God, and "Mind of God," and the Lord God formed man from the dust of the earth and breathed into his nostrils the breath of life, and man became a living soul.

Neshamah, the breath of life, is the principle of life that is called "Lord's Lamp" in the Bible because the moral sense is a direct gift from God and enables man to see his real condition.

Proverbs 20:27 words of truth reports: "The Spirit of man is the candle of the Lord, searching all the inward parts of the belly" and Ec. 12:7 tells us that "Then shall the dust return to the earth as it was the spirit shall return unto God who gave it."

Adam, after nine hundred thirty years of life on earth, finally died then and only then did the breath of God return back to God.

Everything that has life breathes. Plants may not have lungs as mammals do, but they definitely breathe, taking in the toxins we release when we exhale and producing pure air. God breathes his words of life while inhaling and exhaling, producing life, giving instruction. He changes the course of man, roads, and continents to include the heavens, rearranging the stars and creating a new universe as He speaks all into and out of existence. We also in death return the breath that was given freely back to God, which is generated power given to a newborn creation of God.

When God speaks, His breath forms and produces the Words that form nothing become something as we have seen in the beginning of His creation power of the heavens and earth, "and the spirit of God moved on the face of the waters." And God said, "Let there be light," and there was light, a firmament in the midst of the waters. He called for dry land, and it was so. He formed the earth and separated the land from the seas, and the earth brought forth grass, hereby yielding seed and fruit trees. God created all of the pleasures we enjoy today. Paul, in his writing to the Philippines, tells us to "Have this attitude within yourselves, which is also in Christ Jesus, who although He existed in the form of God did not regard equality with God, a thing to be grasped, but emptied himself, taking the form of a bond servant and being made in the likeness of man."

Most importantly, God's gift of the Holy Spirit, a resurrected Jesus, is all about his calling that caused our Savior, to rise up and brought unto us a new redeeming breath of salvation.

Being found in appearance as a man, He humbled himself by becoming obedient to the point of death, even death on a wooden cross. Therefore, also God highly exalted Him and bestowed on Him the name that is above every name, and at the name of Jesus every knee shall bow and every tongue will confess that He, Jesus, is Lord; to the glory of God the Father.

Jesus starts out as God, as he has always been, what He only could be. He poured out Himself and died to His Godliness, to be born to his Humanity. He then lived His life as a human and upon the cross died to his humanity, not my will but thy will be done. At that point, He was reborn to His Godliness. God dies that we might live, that we die from our old sins and be regenerated into life, destined for eternity.

God dies to himself, and our humanity is born. The attributes of God are those fundamental and necessary qualities of his nature, which form the grounds for his various manifestations to his creations. God's absolute attributes that reveal and affect the inner being of God and his relationship to himself, which is independent of his relationship with the universe. By God's relative attributes, we see a relationship that is too related to the outward relationship of Him to the universe, which he created.

We see the work of God's creation as he exhales into existence his free will in art form, making all things by mere words of his power and without any previous material. This is the breath of God, which is the cycle of the universe. The earth and galaxies are created all in the presence of the breath of God.

The oceans contain uncountable drops of water. In presence of the light, that water evaporates and forms into clouds. The clouds then collect all of the individual droplets of water based on the correct temperature over and in the clouds. Rainwater will drop back to earth and will find its way back to the ocean.

This is the breath of God. It is true that the heavens do declare the glory of God, and the Earth does show His handiwork. God's nature and attributes can be clearly seen through what he has made. God is the ocean; we are the raindrops. The ocean dies to itself to become a raindrop again, and the raindrops die to themselves to be reborn as an ocean once again.

We see this clearly in the book of Philippians as being Jesus' pathway. Jesus, having dwelt in Godliness, emptied himself out to become a member of humanities, society, empting himself of himself again to resume being Godliness. It is emphatically clear throughout the Bible that Jesus' pathway and his life is a blueprint for ours.

Before God created the heavens and earth, we were apart and remained inside the Master's plans for salvation. He knew each and every one of us even before we were formed in our mother's womb, so God created us and placed us here at this appointed time. He breathed into the nostrils of Adam and Eve the breath of life, and they became a living soul. We then live our lives encased in ego.

Eventually we come to the point where we can say, "No longer my will; my small, limited, egocentric human will be done," but rather, "Heavenly Father, thy will be done." We take up our old wooded cross, and we join the living Christ in a life of eternal praise and worship unto God. We can then say that we, as small, individual raindrops, no longer exist. It is Christ Jesus who lives in us. We have rejoined the ocean. We are now one with the Heavenly Father, and He pours through and expresses himself in and around us.

This is not the end; you do not want to spend the rest of eternity in your small, limited human world. There are realms of glory beyond your wildest comprehension. That was when we responded to the call of God, and we, as in likeness of Jesus, became obedient to the point of death, even death on that old wooden cross.

His spirit is within us, surrounding us, embracing our spiritual soul. He exalts us and raises us up into heaven to be with him, to surround the heavenly throne so that he might say to us, "Well done, my good and faithful servants." This is the breath of the living God working in ordinary people as we serve an extraordinary God.

The fundamental article of the Christian faith is this God is the creator. In this statement, a Christian Biblical religious doctrine of being is opposed to all forms of ontology. Its main thesis is that all beings are either God's or have been created and established by him. But the Biblical ontology is not content with this. It states that God has created all that is outside Himself through his word. The Word of God is the breath of God, which forms the words that come from His mouth.

The Word of God, therefore, according to the teaching of the Bible, is the grounds of being of all created existence, not merely in the sense that all created beings have their origin in the Word of God, but in the sense that in the word all things cohere. "70: For by Him all things were created that are in heaven and that are in earth, visible and invisible, whether they be thrones or dominions or principalities or powers. All things were created through Him and for Him" (Col. 1:16).

Man has quite a special relationship of being to the Word of God, because in man being and perception stand in a peculiar relationship to one another.

His voice speaks from the book of Colossians 1:16; "All things were made by Him, and without Him was not anything made that was made" (John 1:9). But only of man is it said that this word is also the light, the true light, which lightest every man.

The specific being of man, which distinguishes him from all other creatures, is not only known from the breath of God but is also based upon the Word of God since all created existence is based upon the breath and Word of God.

Man is man by the fact that he is a creature who stands in a special relationship to the breath of God, a relationship of being grounded in and upheld by the word who is being the brightness of His glory and the express image of His person, and upholding all things by the word of His power, when He had by Himself purged our sins and sat down at the right hand of the Majesty on high (Hebrews 1:3).

This is no mere phrase or figure of speech but a simple and realistic expression of the mouth of God. Just as the new man is generated by the breath and Word of God, so also the original man in the divine original act of creation was generated by the breath and Word of God.

Just as this generation in the Word of God included the hearing of the Word of God and belief in the Word and thus a spiritual relationship to the Word of God, so also the original creation includes such a process, which makes man not merely a product but a receiver of the divine word.

The meaning of all responsibility is love, for love is the fulfilling of all law. Man can only be understood as being created from the love of God. Love is both the source and the meaning of his life. Again, every human being is aware of this to some extent, even if only dimly, but what he cannot and does not know for himself is why this is so with the real content of the revelation of God in Jesus Christ. Only in this revelation is the meaning of the words "Love rightly," defined for us by the divine action, and in it alone is this love revealed to us as the ground and the end of our life. In it we perceive why, to whom, and for what purpose we are responsible. We understand ourselves in the light of the divine love even in our very godlessness. For only we understand that godlessness and lovelessness are the same things. The being of man has its ground in the being, the will, and the works of God.

The Breath
of God Inspiration Method

Inspiration is a divine influence or action on a person held to qualify him to receive and communicate sacred revelation, the act of drawing in, specifically the drawing of air into the lungs, an inspiring agent or influence. One of the greatest inspiring individuals I have ever met was my mother, Mrs. Geneva Harrell. She lived her life as a person who did all she could to protect her children, to ensure they attended school and church, and influenced me to set and achieve higher goals in life. She was born as a twin, and at birth her twin sister was called by God to return home. My grandmother, whom I did not meet, was Mrs. Ellen Brown Harrell, who also took her last breath and died in 1924.

My earthly father was unknown to me. My mother's reluctance to tell me anything about him always made me feel that he abandoned us, but I always had hope that one day he would return to find his first son and reclaim my mother as his wife.

At a young age, I always felt that God had something special for me to do. I was slow in learning and was shy when it came to social events, mainly because of my dark complexion. The shades of racism that existed among the Negros during those times were all based on the complexion of one's skin. Children in school would call me "Mighty Joe Young," after the movies about a giant ape. I would have fought them all, but I was a Christian and was very obedient to my mother's words of instruction until I moved out of the house. Called and called again, in accordance to the Bible, God "calls" or summons people to do certain things. In a general sense, God calls all men to receive the salvation and redemption that can be found only in His Son, Jesus Christ. After we have answered the call to salvation and received Jesus Christ as Lord God, He will continue to call us to other tasks that are moral in nature and affect a believer's attitude and conduct. He calls believers to fellowship with Christ, to holiness, to liberty, to peace, to virtue. A believer is to walk worthy of the calling they have received.

I joined the United States Army and felt as if I was running from God. I often challenged myself while stationed in Germany. I remained faithful unto God and did not develop a spirit of contradictions, shame, and pride. I was weak in my relations with God. I wanted to end it all but couldn't. Each time I did what I felt was right, it failed. Only after being awakened by God as I went through many storms did I see that I could not make it without him. I developed a spirit of repentance and made a personal amalgamation with God that I would serve him until I died. Praise God, I have not forfeited in any way. Mr. Timothy Morton in his book, called *Into the Ministry*, agrees that for many believers, one of the most difficult and elusive things encountered is determining the will of God for one's life. For some they seem to know the path God would have them travel but hesitate to follow it. For me I did not know, but He began to lead and I followed. I attended and became a member of the Sharon Baptist Church of greater New Brunswick, NJ. While reading, studying my Bible, and attending Sunday school, I felt him pulling me in the direction of teaching His divine words, and after fasting, praying, and counseling, I became a Sunday school teacher for the children, but I felt spiritual and more at ease with the adults. A stronger desire came over me for furthering my education. "Which way, Lord?" was my question to God as I finished my undergraduate course and applied for a master's degree in social work. I was confused and felt I had missed the mark God wanted me to follow. So I applied to the New Brunswick Theological Seminary and attended one year, until I ran out of money. The desire for more knowledge in God's words forced me to find a substitute. I was led to the Word Harvest Bible Institute and remained there until they closed the doors due to a lack of funds. God opened another door for me to attend the Central Bible Institute, located in Piscataway, New Jersey, under the spiritual leadership of Rev. Dr. Cora Smithson, where I obtained my master's in theology. During the transformation period, I was elevated to reverend and now stand ready for further instructions from God. My desire is to become a pastor of one of His churches.

I was not reaching for this calling and as a child felt something inside pulling at me. I was a drunkard and attempted to find the love lost by my father's abandonment, and God ensured that he was with me and His love for me would cover me.

He developed an inspirational method, which not only demonstrated the love for the divine touch, breathe in that divine inspiration, and do, create, and inspire. He gives the definition of the word "inspiration" as the breath of God. Whether you are religious or not, the idea of God or a little god or a muse breathing inspiration into the depths of our beings is a beautiful one. Even if the world is naught but a natural miracle, this idea can lift you up and give you the spark of life to "do" something great.

That's inspiration at its absolute best, not just when it lifts us up, makes us feel good or enthusiastic or excited, but when it "moves" us, when we become so moved that we create something to truth or beauty.

It is an elusive thing, this pure inspiration, something people of all types of creativity seek on a daily basis.

The Breath of God:
Identifying Spiritual Energy

Mr. Stenger addresses in his book, *The Breath of God: Identifing Spiritual Energy*, identifies abstracts of energy exit beyond those recognized by physics, these should be detectable in controlled experiments by the observation of apparent violation of energy conservation. This includes by the psychic associated with paranormal phenomena, the vital energies supposedly manipulated in alternative.

Medicine, supernatural, or spiritual energy. So all of the data is consistent with conservation of the known forms of energy. Furthermore, observations indicate that the total energy of the universe is zero, and so no outsider energy was necessary to bring it about.

Energy and spirit: The English word "energy" comes from the Greek "energies," for "activity."

Webster's Dictionary gives 1599 as the earliest date for its use, but energy did not play an identifiable role in physics until 1847. At that time, Helmholtz introduced the law of conservation of energy, also known as the first law of thermodynamics, which has proven to be one of the most powerful principles of physics.

Most people presume that life and consciousness require some activating agent beyond cold, impersonal matter. I suppose it would be consistent with the root of their term to call this a kind of energy. However, what is being proposed by paranormal lists appears to be a little different from the traditional notions of "spirit" or "soul." This strikes me as yet another example of an old idea being given a new life, a scientific-sounding name to make it sound like something new and give it modern authority.

Modern super-naturalists seem to be saying that they can feel the "Breath of God" upon their cheeks. Although many skeptics prefer not to bring religion into the discussions of paranormal claims, a connection between religion and the paranormal is impossible to avoid because of the connection with the supernatural, either direct or implied. No matter how much the editors of skeptical publications may wish to avoid offending potential subscribers, science and religion are two "magisterials" that cannot help but overlap when discussing paranormal claims.

Many of the original paranormal researchers, such as Oliver Lodge, William Crookes, and Joseph Banks Rhine, seem to have had strong religious motivations for their efforts to demonstrate the reality of psychic phenomena. I suspect many of the current investigators have similar motivations and that much of their mostly private funding is donated in the hope of "proving" religious belief. The religious overtones of astrology, UFO-logy, alien abductions, and much of alternative medicine are also evident.

If the existence of ESP could be shown, then this would be interpreted by many as evidence for the long-sought spiritual element to the universe. Although natural explanations would still have to be ruled out, these are not very likely to be found based on what we already know about the physical universe. Psychic energy is not part of the current standard model, and no conceivable extension makes any room for it.

Jacob Behmen (Jakob Boehme), 1575-1624, the *Teutonic Theosopher* article was brought forth in the 1600s by a humble German shoemaker, translated into English over one hundred years later, suppressed, and hidden away until recently in theological archives around the world.

Mr. Behmen opened his article with a statement: "How he that earnestly seek salvation, must suffer himself to be brought out of the confused and contention Babel, by the Spirit of Christ, that he may be born anew in the Spirit of Christ and live to Him only."

Unlike Victor J. Stenger, the psychic who writes about the energy and spirit found in the universe, Mr. Behmen strangely believed and writes about the regeneration spirit of our God. Moses said God created man in his image, in the image of God created in him. This we understand to be both out of the eternal and temporal Birth, out of the inward and Spiritual Word, which he breathed into him, into the created image, and then out of the substance of the inward spiritual World, which is Holy.

For as there is a Natural and Substance in the outward world, so also in the inward spiritual world there is a Natural and Substance that is spiritual, from which the outward world is breathed forth and produced out of light and darkness and created to have a beginning and time. And out of the substance of the inward and outward world was created out of and in the likeness of the birth of all substance. The body is a "Limbus," of the earth, and also a Limbus of the heavenly substance, for the earth is breathed for, outspoken, or created out of Limbus, an extract or a kind of seed, which contains all that which the thing from whence it is taken hath the darkness and light world. In the word "Fiat viz." in the eternal desire, man was taken out of the earth and created an image out of time and eternity.

This image was in the inward and spiritual element, from whence the four elements proceed and are produced. In Paradise, for the properties of nature from the fire-dark-and-light world were all in harmony and agreement in numbers, weight, and measure. One of them was not manifested more eminently than another, neither was there any strife or contrariety among the powers and properties.

Into the created image of God breathed the Spirit and breath of understanding out of the three worlds, as one only soul which, as to its original principle or essence, is or consists the inward dark-fire-world of the eternal spiritual nature, according to which God called himself a strong, jealous God and a consuming fire.

And this now is the eternal creaturely great soul, a magical breath of fire, in which fire consists in the original life form the great power of separation. God's anger, or the eternal darkness, is in this property, so far as fire reached without giving light.

The second property of the breath of God is the spirit of the source of light, proceeding from the great fiery desire of love, from the great meekness, according to which God called himself a loving, merciful God, in which consists the true spirit of understanding and of life on power.

For as light shines from power, and as the power of the understanding is discerned in the light, so the breath of the light was joined to the breath of the fire of God and breathed into the image of man.

The third property of the breath of God was the outward air with its constellation or Astrum, wherein the life and constellation of the outward substance and body did consist. This breathed into his nostrils, and as time and eternity hang together and as time is produced out of eternity, so the inward breathed of God hung to the outward.

This threefold soul was at once breathed into man, and each substance of the body received the spirit according to its property. The outward flesh received the air and its constellation, for a rational and vegetative life, to the manifestation of the wonders of God, and the light body or heavenly substance received the breath of the light of the great divine powers and virtues, which breath is called the Holy Spirit (Ghost).

The light pieced through the darkness, viz. through the dark breath of fire, and also through the breath of the outward air and its constellation or Astrum, and so deprived all the properties of their power, that neither the anguish of the breath of fire in the inward property of the soul, nor heat or cold, or any of all the properties of the outward constellation, might or could be manifested.

The properties of all of the three worlds in soul and body were in equal agreement, temperature, and weight. That which was inward and holy ruled through and over the outward, that is, the outward parts of the outward life, of the outward stars and constellations and four elements, and that original and universal power of the inward over the outward constituted the holy paradise.

God/Man was both in heaven and also in the outward world and was Lord over all creations and creatures of this world. Nothing could concur or destroy him, for such was the earth until the blessing of God came forth. The holy property of the spiritual world sprung up through the earth and brought forth the holy paradise called "Eden," producing fruits that man could eat in a spiritual, paradisiacal manner.

Man was created in the image and likeness of God in that respect, according to time and eternity, out of body time and eternity, yet in and for an immortal life, which was without enmity or contrariety.

Satan (the devil), having himself been a prince and hierarch in the place of this world and cast out for his pride into the dark, anguishing, painful, and hostile property and source, brought into the wrath of God, envied man the glory of being created in and for the spiritual world, the place he himself once possessed, and therefore brought his imagination or desires into the image of man and made it so lusting (desiring) that the curiosity, the cancer of dark world, and accompany with the outward world rose in man, and departed from the equal agreement and temperature wherein they stood, and so one predominated over the other.

Both properties were separately made manifested itself, and each of them produced pride and lusted at which was in common likeness of itself. That which was created from a dark world, the (dust of the earth), which was born from the light of the world, would eat of the Limbus of the earth, according to its own desires; at this juncture, good and evil had manifested into Adam.

Tasting and seeing produced the desire to eat the properties that grow out of the earth, from whence the properties of the body were extracted then and that drew such a branch out of the earth, the eating of such properties causing an awakened vanity.

For the spirit of the strong and great supernatural power (the Holy Spirit) of eternity was breathed into Adam, from whom the earth with its properties was also breathed forth by the (Word) of God; the fiat viz., a strong desire for eternal life, it become the attracting, the essence of the earth. God's divine wisdom distancing the tree of knowledge of good and evil, Adam the man must be tried to see whether he would stand and subsist in his own powers, before the tempter (Satan) and before the wrath of the eternal nature and whether the soul would continue in the equal agreement of the properties in true resignation under the spirit of God as an instrument of God's harmony, a tuned instrument of divine joyfulness and love for the spirit of God to strike upon. This tested and tried by the tree, and this severe commandment was given to Adam: "Thou shall not eat thereof, for on that day thou eat of it, thou shall surely die."

Moses writes in verse Genesis 2:18; 21; 22: 79: Then the Lord God said, 'It is not good for the man to be alone. I will make a helper as his complement.' 21: So the Lord God caused a deep sleep to come over the man, and he slept. God took one of his ribs and closed the flesh at that place. 22: Then the Lord God made the rib He had taken from the man into a woman and brought her to the man."

The author suggests man would not continue in the obedience of the divine harmony in the properties, submitting himself to stand still as an instrument of the spirit of God; therefore, God suffered him to fall from the divine harmony into a harmony of his own. Adam was to be awakening into the properties of good and evil. Introduced into the article is the author's interpretation, that while Adam was in this sleep he died from the Angelical World and fell under the power of the outward fiat, and thus bade farewell to the eternal image, which was of God's begetting. Of course, it's pointed that while he, Adam, slept, God fiat and divine power caused a transformation of change to the body of Adam. Adam's Angelical world was what sustained him while under this deep sleep induced by God. So the outward world touched nothing of the soul of Adam, the inward spirit world, which was regenerated again and caused no pain or need for a recovery period. Adam remained as a begotten son of God.

And then by the fiat, God made the woman out of him, out of the Matrix of Venus, viz. out of that property wherein Adam had the begetters in himself, and so out of one body God made two and divided the properties of the tinctures, viz. the properties of the watery and fiery souls.

Genesis 2:23: "And the man said: this one, at last, is bone of my bone and flesh of my flesh; this one will be called 'woman,' for she was taken from man." The mixture of tincture and water, which produced a color fused together with fire. The ingredients fused together produced light, a pure blinding light where it houses the Holy Spirit. So the woman has also received the inward spirit of God by His breath, which produces life.

From Adam a rib was taken, and also taken was his genetic makeup. His desire of self-love was formed into the woman in accordance of his likeness. Recorded in Genesis 2:24: "This is why a man leaves his father and mother and bonds with his wife, and they become one flesh." Both the man and his wife were naked, yet felt no shame.

Tinctures: 1: to tint or stain with color; 2: to infuse or install with a property or entity; IMPREGENATE: to imbues with a quality.

God's commands found in Genesis 1:28: "God blessed them, and God said to them, 'Be fruitful, multiply, fill the earth, and subdue it rule the fish of the sea, the birds of the sky, and every creature that crawls on the earth.'"

God has established a covenant with His first creation of male and female and gave instructions to "be fruitful and multiply." This same mandate applies to His second creations, Adam and Eve. Yes! Adam saw himself in the creation of himself and female, whom he named, and the ceremony of matrimony was conducted by the creator himself. Adam desired Eve, and Eve desired Adam.

Satan, who has been banished from heaven, separated from the presence of God until summoned to the celestial council, fell to the earth and in his darkened spirit of pride seeks and watches over human affairs and brings with the object searching out men's sins and accusing them in the celestial court. He is thus invested with a certain malevolent and malignant character, but it is to be observed that he has no power to act without the Divine permission being first obtained and cannot, therefore, be regarded as the embodiment of the power that opposes the Deity.

Genesis 3:1: "Now the serpent was the most cunning of all the wild animals that the Lord God had made. He said to the woman, 'Did God really say, "You can't eat from any tree in the Garden"?'"

In the book of Wisdom (2:24), by the envy of the devil, death entered into the world. We already met with the identification of the serpent of Gen. 3 with Satan, who afterward becomes a fixed element in belief, and an allusion to the same idea may be detected in the Psalm of Solomon, where the prosperous wicked man is said to be "like a serpent, to pervert wisdom, speaking with the words of transgressors." The same identification also meets us in the book of the Secrets of Enoch (ft century A.D.), where, moreover, Satanology shows a rich development (the pride, revolt, and fall of Satan are dwelt upon). Cf. art. Fall.

It could have been the first desire of Eve that she might eat of the tree of vanity, of evil and good, to which the devil in the form of a serpent persuaded her, saying that her eyes should be opened and should be as God himself, which was both a lie and a truth.

But he told her not that she should lose the divine light and power, thereby he only said her eyes should be opened, that she might taste, prove, and know evil and good, as he had done. Neither did he tell her that heat and cold would awaken in her and that the property of the outward constellations would have great power over the flesh and over the mind.

His only aim was that the angelical image viz. the substance, which came from the inward spiritual world, might disappear in them. For then they would be constrained to live in subjection to the gross earthliness and the constellations or stars, and that he knew. Well enough that when the outward world perished, the soul would be with him in darkness. For he saw that the body must die, which he perceived by that which God had intimated, and so he expected still to be Lord to all eternity in the place of this world, in his false shape, which he had gotten, and therefore he seduced man.

For when Adam and Eve were eating the fruit, evil and good entered into the body, then the imagination of the body received vanity in the fruit, and then vanity awaked in the flesh, and the dark world got the upper hand and dominion in the vanity of the earthliness, upon which the fair image of heaven that proceeded out to the heavenly divine world instantly disappeared.

Here Adam and Eve died to the kingdom of heaven and awakened to the Outward World, and then the fire soul, as it stood in love of God, disappeared as to the Holy Power, virtue, and property, and instead thereof the wrathful anger, viz. the dark-fire world, awakened in it, and so the soul became in one part, viz. in the inward nature, a half-devil, and in the outward part as related to the outward world a beast.

Here are bounds of death and the gates of hell, for which because God became man that he might destroy death, defeat the devil's purpose, and change hell into great love again.

Let this be told unto you: Ye children of men. it was said unto you, at the sound of a trumpet that you should instantly go forth from the abominable vanity for the fire thereof burn. The author of this article is unknown. His topic is "There Is a First, and There Is a Second." He opens with 1 Cor. 15:44-49. There the Apostle Paul is explaining to us the definitive law of the Bible interpretation, which is: "The first is always the physical and the second is always the Spiritual."

Soul-ish body; it is raised a spiritual body. There is a natural soul-ish body, and there is a spiritual body. And so it is written, the first Adam was made a living soul (a soul is a living being that has five senses); the last Adam (Christ) was made a life-giving Spirit.

Howbeit that was not first which is spiritual, but that which is natural (the spiritual is never first. The natural or physical always first), and afterward that which is spiritual (the spiritual is always second).

"Soul-ish," noun; soul; the spiritual principle embodied in human beings, all rational and spiritual beings, or the universe. "Ish," adjective, suffix; of relating to being chiefly in nationally or ethnic groups. "Soul-ish" means it can be detected with the five senses.

The first man, Adam, is of the earth, earthly (made of dust, the natural); the second man is the Lord from heaven (Jesus Christ, the spiritual) (1 Cor. 15:44-47). The first is the earthly or natural. The second is the spiritual, meaning that it cannot be detected by the five senses, but only detected by spiritual knowledge, revelation knowledge, as a result of God putting His disposition in us.

First man, Adam: earthly or natural. "The first man is of earth, earthly." Second Man, Jesus, Spiritual, "the last Adam was made a quickening (life-giving) spirit" (1 Cor. 15:47). The first birth: earthly or natural. A natural, physical birth can be detected with the five senses. It can be seen, heard, touched. The second birth (being born again): Spiritual. A spiritual rebirth cannot be detected by using the five senses. It is a spiritual phenomenon.

That which is born of the flesh is flesh (physical, earthly, natural), and that which is born of the spirit (breath) is spirit (breath) (John 3:6). "If I have told you earthly things (things you can understand with your five senses). And you believe not, how shall you believe if I tell you of heavenly things? Things that require revelation is knowledge to understand" (John 3:12).

"For Christ also has once suffered for sins, the just and for the unjust, that he might bring us to God, being put to death in the flesh, but quickened (given life) by the Spirit."

First death: Earthly or natural, the death that we naturally die, "the death" that is in us from the moment we are born. As soon as we are born, we begin to die.

The five senses: sight, touch, taste, smell, and hear, are the source of all knowledge. However, the senses can only grasp physical, material things. And the senses may become impaired by accident, carelessness, overwork, or dissipation; they are not to be depended upon. They are not absolutely true.

The second death: spiritual death to sin, the old man of sin is crucified; we are created a new creature in Christ Jesus.

The First Breath vs. the Second Breath

The first breath has been identified as being that of "God the Father," who in the beginning created heaven and earth. The second breath in which we will discuss is that of our Lord and Savior "Jesus Christ." The breath in which we are speaking about is the third person of the Trinity, the "Holy Spirit."

God the Father has been the title given to Him in the twentieth-century Baptist churches. Theologians, historians, and scholars have identified other names that paint and describe the great sovereignty of God. The existence of God is everywhere assumed in the sacred volume; it will not, therefore, be necessary here to consider the arguments adduced to show that the belief in God's existence is reasonable. Fact, that for the ungodly man say there is no God, but the doubtless is, not that existence of God is denied, but that the "fool" alleges that God does not concern Himself with man. In the pride of their countenance, the wicked say, "God will not seek it out"; all of their thoughts are": "There is no God." God revealed Himself by divers' portions and in divers' manners. The world only gradually acquired the knowledge of God, which we now possess, and it is therefore a gross mistake to look for our ideas and standards of responsibility in the early ages of mankind.

The names of God found in the Old Testament: Elohim is the ordinary Hebrew name for God, a plural word of doubtful origin and meaning. It is used as an ordinary plural, of heathen gods or of supernatural beings. Eloah, which we find in the book of Job, is also found in poetry and in late prose. El

Shaddai: The meaning of Shaddai is uncertain; the name has been derived from a root meaning "to overthrow" and would then mean "the Destroyer" or from a root meaning "to pour" and would then mean the "Rain-giver," or it has been interpreted as "my Mountain" or "my Lord." EI Elyon: "God Most High," found in Genesis 14:17-20. The action of Abram is seen by Melchizedek, who gave honor unto the "God Most High." Elyon is also found alone, as in Psalm 82:6: "I have said, Ye are gods; and all of you are children of the Most High" (Psalm 57:2). I will cry unto God Most High, unto God that performeth all things for me.

Adonai (Lord), a title common in the prophets, expressing dependence, as of a servant on his master of a wife on her husband. Jehovah, Yahweh are usually written Jahweh, which may be a prehistorical name.

When God Himself speaks, He uses the first person and the name becomes "I Am" or "I Will Be." It denotes then existence, yet it is understood as expressing active and self-manifesting. "But the king said to her, 'Don't be afraid. What do you see?' 'I see a spirit form coming up out of the earth,' the woman answered" (Hebrews 28:13, KJV), or even the earthly judges; God has taken His place in the divine assembly; He judges among the gods: "2: How judges among the gods unjustly and show partiality to the wicked? 3: Provide justice for the needy and the fatherless; uphold the rights of the oppressed and the destitute. 4: Rescue the poor and needy; save them from the power of the wicked." They do not know or understand; they wander in darkness. All the foundations of the earth are shaken. "6: I said, ';You are gods; you are all sons of the Most High. 7: However, you will die like men and fall like any other ruler.' 8: Rise up, God, judge the earth, for all the nations belong to you" (Psalm 82:1-8, KJV).

Traditionally it is rendered "God Almighty," and there is perhaps a reference to this sense of the name in the words "He that is mighty." Because the Mighty One has done great things for me and His name is holy (Luke 1:49, KJV). After Abram returned from defeating Chedorlaomer and the kings who were with him, the king of Sodom went out to meet him in the valley of Shaveh (the king's valley). Then Melchizedek, king of Salem, brought out bread and wine. He was a priest to God Most High. He blessed him and said, "Abram is blessed by God Most High, Creator of the heaven and earth, and I gave praise to God Most High who has handed over your enemies to you." "I am or I will be." It denotes, then, existence, yet it is understood as expressing active and self-manifesting existence. It is almost equivalent to "He who has life in Himself." "9: For as the Father hath life in himself; so hath he given to the Son to have life in Himself."

He is also known as "El Shaddai" and "Jehovah," which is the modern and hybrid form dating only from A.D. 1518. The name "Jahweh" was so sacred that it was not, in later Jewish times, pronounced at all, perhaps owing to an over-literal interpretation of the Third Commandment.

Jesus Christ (Immanue1), there is no historical task that is more important than to set forth the life and teaching of Jesus Christ, and none to which it is so difficult to do justice. The importance of the theme is sufficiently attested by the fact that it is felt to be His due to reckon a new era from the date of His birth. From the point of view of Christian faith, there is nothing in time worthy to be set beside the deeds and the words of one who is adored as God manifest in the flesh and the Savior of the World.

The Gospel according to Mark is the oldest of the four canonicals. Beginning with the baptism of Jesus, it gives a sketch of His public ministry, with specimens of His teaching, and carries the narrative to the morning of the resurrection. This Gospel supplies most of our knowledge of the life of Jesus, but its main concern is to bring out the inner meaning and the religious value of His story.

The Gospel of Matthew is now usually regarded as a second and enlarged edition of an Apostolic original. The earlier version, known as the Logia on the grounds of a note of Papias, was a collection of the memorabilia of Jesus. As the Logia consisted mainly of the sayings of our Lord, the later editor combined it with the narrative of Mark in order to supply a more complete picture of the ministry and at the same time added fresh material from independent sources.

In the Gospel according to Luke, it is also dependent on Mark for the general framework and derives from the original Matthew a large body of the teaching. It follows a different authority from Matthew for the nativity and to some extent goes its own way in the history of the Passion while the great interpolation made in part from its special source forms a priceless addition to the synoptic material.

Luke approached his task in a more consciously scientific spirit than his predecessors and recognized an obligation to supply dates and to sketch in the political background of the biography. But for him also, the main business of the historian was to emphasize the religious significance of the event and by that exhibiting Jesus as the Savior of the world, the Friend of sinners. He is especially interested as the companion and disciple of Apostle Paul, incidents and sayings that illustrate the graciousness and the universality of the Gospel.

Prominence is given to the rejection of Jesus by Nazareth and Jerusalem and to His discovery among the Gentiles of the faith for which He sought. It is also characteristic that Luke gives a full account of the beginnings of the missionary activity of the Church.

He (Jesus) publicly claims to be the Messiah. "If thou art the Christ, tell us plainly." Jesus answered them, "I told you and ye believed not." There is also developed a high doctrine of his original and primordial dignity. He is from God. He is before Abraham and the Father is One, which lastly is interpreted to mean that being a man He makes Himself God. Proportional to His dignity are the blessings that He bestows, repose and refreshment of the soul's true life, spiritual freedom resurrected, and life everlasting.

"The Holy Spirit," which is the third person of the Trinity of God, is the breath of God and of the Son. The Christian doctrine of the Holy Spirit arises out of the experience of the Church as it interprets and is itself interpreted by the promise of the Comforter given by Jesus to His disciples. This appeal to experience follows the method adopted by Apostle Peter in his Pentecostal sermon.

The Holy Spirit is God, a Person within the Godhead, the Third Person, the knowledge of whom depends on the revelation of the Father and Son, from both of whom He proceeds. He was in the world and spoke by the prophets before the Word became flesh and was Himself the agent in that creative act. Through Him the atonement was consummated. He is the life-giving presence within the universal Church, the Divine agent in its sacramental and authoritative acts, communicating Himself as a presence and power to the individual Christian, mediating to him forgiveness and new birth, nourishing, increasing, and purifying his whole personality, kittling him into the fellowship of saints, and finally, through the resurrection of body, bringing him to the fullness of eternal life.

The Lord formed his second creation out of the dust of the earth and breathed into his nostrils, and he became a living soul, meaning man was alive and was embedded with the five senses: hearing, tasting, smelling, seeing, and touching, a specialized animal function or mechanism as sight, hearing, smell, taste, or touch basically involving a stimulus and a sense organ. This action of love can be interpreted in the creation of Eve as God created her from one rib taken from Adam. Before life was even awarded, God's breath of life was once again breathed into her.

In the book of Genesis, even before God created man in His image, He, with the help from the Word of God and the Holy Spirit, created heaven and earth; on the sixth day after God created man in His own image, he blessed them. Everything having the breath of life in it, He has given every green plant for food. "And it was so." And it was very good. Evening came and then morning of the sixth day.

Conformation of His use of His breath to create all that walk, crawl, or fly has his spirit of life within them. Oddly enough, the very substance of life is a commodity we cannot see. We cannot feel unless it moves, we cannot smell it unless a foreign commodity is in it, and we cannot hear it and still we cannot live without it. It is our life. We can live without it in the womb as we get the alternating current from our moms, but outside the womb we need that breath of life.

All animals receive the breath of life from God Most High. All animals except man are complete, or innocent and blameless. However, man is the only animal that can receive the Holy Spirit. And once he receives the Holy Spirit he is holy, complete, and innocent, as are the other animals.

Considering man was meant to be made in the image of God, we hopefully agree that there is still some finishing work to be done. " If you love me, you will keep my commands. 16: And I will ask the Father and He will give you another Counselor to be with you forever. 17: He is the Spirit of truth. The world is unable to receive Him because it doesn't see Him or know Him. But you do know him because He remains with you and will be in you. 18: I will not leave you as orphans; I am coming to you."

The Holy Spirit would be given to those who keep His commandments. The Holy Spirit cannot be received by any animal and only by those of the human animal race who love Him and humble themselves. Another name for the Holy Ghost is the Comforter, and he comes not from Christ but from the Father. He is a teacher, and he is a guide or a leader. He, in a sense, is our memory, for he brings to our remembrance all we need to know. Neither is He served by human hands, as though He needed anything, since He Himself gives everyone life and breath and all things. From one man He has made every nationality to live over the whole earth and has determined their appointed times and the boundaries of where they live. He did this so they might seek God, and perhaps they might reach out and find Him, though He is not far from each one of us. For in Him we live and move and exist as even some of your own poets have said, "For we are also His offspring." Being God's offspring, then, we shouldn't think that his divine nature is like gold or silver or stone, an image fashioned by human art and imagination.

There are two words in the Greek language that mean life: "Psuche" and "Zoe." Psuche is used to denote the physical life we live on this earth. But whenever the term "eonian" (mistranslated "eternal") life is used, it is the Greek word "Zoe."

We have a physical life (psuche), maintained by physical breath, the breath that God breathed into Adam's nostrils. And we have spiritual life.

1Zoe is the life of Christ in us (eonian life), maintained by Spiritual Breath, God's breath of Holiness. The first life physical life is psuche in the Greek, the second life, "spiritual life" (eonian) life, the life of Christ manifested in us, is Zoe in the Greek.

Physical life is "psuche" in the Greek: "Therefore I say unto you, do not worry about your life, what you shall eat, or what you shall drink, nor yet for your body, what you shall put on. Is not the life more than food and the body more than raiment?" (Matthew 6:25). "That whosoever believeth in Him should not perish, but have eternal life" (John 3:15). Whenever the words "eonian life" are used, the Zoe form of the Greek word "life" is used.

The term is used so often that "Holy Spirit" is a mistranslation of the words "Breath of Holiness," which is the second breath. God gives physical breath to sustain physical life. His breath (oxygen) containing his spirit must circulate to every cell in our body to sustain in physical life. God also gives us Spiritual Breath, God's breath of Holiness, which also must circulate throughout every part of us and the universe to sustain and maintain spiritual and physical life. The first breath is physical and the second breath is Spiritual Breath, which means that God's breath is life.

One example we can reach out and form a great picture of the powerful effects of the breath of God is found in the book of Ezekiel 37. Marie Kolasinski writes that God is speaking to Ezekiel about Israel just the way He is speaking to the seed of buried in prison. First he tells Ezekiel to prophesy upon the dry bones, and as he did the bones began to come together, get fat on them, and they began to live as the breath of life came into them.

The amazing thing is this the entire house of Israel coming forth. They got the breath of life and were a living soul, but they cried out to the Lord and said, "Our bones are dried and our hope is lost, and we are cut off from our parts." Then the most awesome thing happened to these who were living souls. He told Ezekiel to prophesy, "This saith the Lord God, 'Behold, oh, my people, I will open your graves and you will know that I am the Lord. And I will put my Spirit in you and ye shall live, the thing that differentiates us from the animal world.'" He completes God's creations of man.

Jesus was resurrected by God. He (Jesus) breathed upon the disciples, and they received the Holy Ghost. They were disciples, they were disciplined. John 20: "But this speaks He of the Spirit, which they that believe in Him should receive; For the Holy Ghost was not yet given, because Jesus was not yet glorified." That believing in Him is the same as following Him to Calvary and becoming the will of God.

The glory of the resurrection is he. God is completing His work with man. The graves are opening, and He is looking upon His creation and it is good. And then God rested from His labor.

The law of sin and death gave way to a fulfillment of promise in the law of the spirit of life, which gives us freedom in Christ Jesus! Jesus personified the Word of God. The Word is Spirit and life. The Spirit is the breath of God! The Hebrew and Greek words for "spirit" indicate breath or wind as a primary characteristic. So Jesus, as the Word, becomes flesh walking the earth, releasing the Spirit of God with every word he spoke, and since he breathed His last breath on the cross the world has never been the same. The "economy of the Trinity" means the different ways the three persons act as they relate to the world and to each other for all eternity. We see these different functions in the work of creation. God the Father spoke the creative words to bring the universe into being. But it was God the Son, the eternal Word of God, who carried out these creative decrees. "All things were made through him and without him was not anything made that was made" (John 1:3). Moreover, "in him all things were created, in heaven and on earth, visible and invisible, weather thrones or dominions or principalities or authorities all things were created through him and for him" (Col. 1:16; Ps. 33:6,9; 1 Col. 8:6; Heb. 1:2).

Mr. Guidry finds Jesus breathed His last breath on the cross; His flesh went from a state of life to death. He believes Jesus' last breath was a final gateway through which the unseen realm began crashing down upon the seen. The earth witnessed the release of something that hadn't been seen since the dawn of creation.

God asks the question to the prophet Ezekiel, "Can these dry bones live?" Jesus answered this question once and for all when he breathed His last! Something happened when Jesus released His last breath. Like the breath of God hovering over the water found in Genesis 1, waiting for a place to rest, Jesus released His breath on the cross and His target was already set.

Jesus shouted again with a loud voice, and gave up His spirit. Suddenly, the curtain of the sanctuary was split into from top to bottom, the earth quaked, and the rocks were split. The tombs were also opened, and many bodies of the saints who had fallen asleep were raised. And they came out of the tombs after His resurrection, entered the holy city, and appeared to many.

The last breath of Jesus demonstrated two factors: 1: that He was the Son of a living God; and 2: He succeeded in establishing a pathway to salvation for all other passages under the I Am.

There was such power released in Jesus' last breath that even the unbeliever, the Roman soldier who was party to His death, declared with certainty, "Surely this was the son of God." The ground shook, rocks spilt, and the veil in the temple was torn forever, adjoining all who walked the path to the access point of the Holy of Holies.

The breath of God in the book of creation gave life to mankind; the breath of Jesus released on the cross gave life to mankind. The breath of the Spirit in Acts 2 poured out His presences on all mankind, and the breath of God grants access. We have the choice to decide what we breathe.

Regeneration is the act of God whereby He cleanses Gospel believers of the defilement of sin, renews their personhoods and the immaterial parts of their human natures (souls-spirit), and imparts to them spiritual life.

Once you take in what has been afforded you by the blood, spirit, or breath of God, you become justified. You are made righteous by faith. There is therefore now no condemnation. Your identity is completely changed. Once a sinner, now a son, flesh corrupted but spirit perfected, Jesus, the one true Judge, has already rendered His verdict: "Not Guilty."

Do You Know Jesus?

The question posed here is "Do you know Jesus?" It is a question that digs deep into the bone. C. W. Emmet gives a description and definition of the word "bone," which is widely used in the Old Testament as a synonym for the body, living or dead, or the person (Psalm 42:10, 51:8). As the solid framework of the body, the bones are the seat of health and strength so that breaking, rottenness, and dryness of the bone are frequent figures for sickness or moral disorder (Proverbs 14:30, 17:22), (Psalm 6:2, 22:14). "Bone of my bone" answers to the English phrase "of the same blood," but the concluding words of Ephesians 5:30 should be omitted. In Luke 24:39, the unique expression seems to emphasize the nature of the resurrection body, as different from the ordinary "flesh and blood." If a person is being called by God to salvation and they yet find themselves producing excuses while remaining standing on a plume line balancing between eternal life or eternal death.

"The doors of the Church are open." Those words, being an invitation into discipleship, are often preached from the pulpits at the end of every church sermon by one of God's anointed ones. From the very beginning, we see the great impact the spirit of regeneration has in and on the individual God is calling. The saving grace through His words and His Spirit reflects God's power of regeneration. First, He has to call or summon the individual to receive salvation and redemption that can only be found in and through His Son, Jesus Christ.

⟨◇⟩

Do You Know Jesus?

Do you know my Jesus? Have you seen Him ride
Seated on a donkey's colt, through the countryside?
People came to greet Him, they waved their branches high
they sang praises to the King of Kings, who was about to die.
Do you know my Jesus? Have you seen Him pray?
In the Garden on His knees, He had but one more day.
For us He bowed His head, for us the drops did flow.
His sweat comes forth as blood His pain we cannot know.
Do you know my Jesus? They put Him on a cross
I could not bear to see Him there, to feel such pain and loss.
The clouds began to darken; the day was turned to night.
His face was hidden from us. He fought with all His might
Do you know my Jesus? They placed Him in a tomb
I did not know if I could live. My world was filled with gloom
But what is this? Oh can it be! He has risen from the dead!
The tomb could not contain Him. We have victory instead!
Hallelujah, Praise the Lord! My Savior lives today!
He has crossed the great divide, He has made a way!
With His blood He paid the price. Our sins have been forgiven!
And by His grace we will spend
Eternity in Heaven!
Do you know my Jesus? Have you heard His call?
Do you walk beside Him? Have you given your all?

A Christian poem by Joan Curtin

⟨◇⟩

One of the early church heresies was Docetism, the belief that Christ had not really become human because of the insurmountable difference between the divine and human world. Some, therefore, thought that Jesus only seemed to be human but actually never gave up his divine nature or essence. At the Council of Chalcedon in A.D. 451, church leaders declared that Jesus was fully God and fully human, a widespread, historical interpretation of Scripture that He was fully human. The Council affirmed that God visited our planet as the Word became flesh and lived among us (John 1:14). They defined the relationship of Christ's two natures as related but without confusion and division. The Jesus I worship is very much God and less a man as seen when Jesus was praying in the Garden of Gethsemane. The Word of God in the flesh dropped to his knees was emotionally depressed, mentally confused, and spiritually overwhelmed. The spirit of obediences pushes Him to the very edge.

Falling to his knees while being in an agony, he prayed more earnestly, and his sweat was as it were great drops of blood falling to the ground (Luke 22:44). This alone confirms the fact that Jesus Christ is God/Man.

When called God we have to respond, to answer His call if we desire to have a loving, everlasting relationship with Him, as we continue to go through the many battles, storms, and temptations Satan will offer to us, if you will! Answering His call requires a strong desire to be set free from the bondage of sin. Regeneration, the rebirth, helps us to recover from the sins that are cursed when we are birthed. "1: And you were dead in your trespasses and sins 2: in which you previously walked according to the ways of this world, according to the ruler who exercises authority over the lower heaven the spirit now working in the disobedient. 3: We too all previously lived among them in our fleshly desires carrying out the inclinations of our flesh and through and we were by nature children under wrath as the others were also, 4: But God, who is rich in mercy, because of His great love that He had for us, 5: made us alive with the Messiah even though we were dead in trespasses. You are saved by the grace 6: together with Christ Jesus. He also raised us up and seated us in the heavens, 7: so that in the coming ages He might display the immeasurable riches of His grace through His kindness to us in Christ Jesus" (Ephesians 2:1-7).

By the grace and mercy of God, man can be called into salvation and obtain that personal relationship with Christ Jesus. Only after His regeneration Spirit is infused in us will we begin to see the wondrous works of God as we inhale His breath and respond to His soft voice that blows through the wind. We begin to seek those things that are the divine attributes in God's nature. We begin to live a life that is pleasing to Him.

Paul specifics that it is God who "made us alive together with Christ" (Eph. 2:5, cf. Col. 2:13). And James says that it is the "Father of Light" (James 1) "of his own will begat he us with the word of truth, that we should be a kind of first fruits of his creatures." Finally, Peter says that God, "according to his abundant mercy has given us new birth through the resurrection of Jesus Christ from the dead" (1 Peter 1:3). Both God the Father and God the Holy Spirit bring about regeneration.

God, not man, is the source of this divine act. It is not by man's works but by God's own good will and pleasure. His great love and free gift, His rich grace and abundant mercy, are the cause of it, and these attributes of God are displayed in the regeneration and conversion of sinners.

Grudem, Wayne "Regeneration": "What does it mean to be born again by a new heart? Also will I give you, and a spirit will I put within you: and I will take away the stony heart out of your flesh, and I will give you and heart of flesh. 27: And I will put my spirit within you, and cause you to walk in my statutes, and ye shall keep my judgments, and do them" (Ezekiel 36:26-27).

As the Gospel comes to us, God speaks through it to summon us to himself and to give us new spiritual life so that we are enabled to respond in faith. Effective calling is thus God the Father speaking powerfully to us, and regeneration is God the Father and God the Holy Spirit working powerfully in us to make us alive. Simultaneously these things will happen as Apostle Peter preached: "While Peter yet spoke these words, the Holy (Spirit) Ghost fell on all them which heard the word" (Acts 10:44, KJV).

What happens in the divine spirit of regeneration? We know that somehow we who were spiritually dead have been made alive to God, and in a very real sense we have been "born again." But we don't understand how it happens or what exactly God does to us to give us this new spiritual life. Jesus says, "The wind blows where it wills, and you hear the sound of it, but you do not know whence it comes or whither it goes; so it is with everyone who is born of the Spirit" (John 3:8). We know that it affects the whole individual. Our spirit is alive to God after regeneration. "10: And if Christ be in you, the body is dead because of sin; but the Spirit it is life because of righteousness" (Romans 8:10, KJV). Mr. Wayne Grudem, in his article "What Does It Mean to Be Born Again?" reports that because regeneration is a work of God within us in which he gives us new life, it is right to conclude that it is an instantaneous event that happens only once. At one moment we are spiritually dead, and then at the next moment we have new spiritual life from God. I agree with him that we know not when it happens when this change occurs, but before this transformation period begins we must have a pure heart and a clean mind.

Jesus, while speaking to Nicodemus, said, "Unless one is born of water and the Spirit, he cannot enter into the kingdom of God" (John 3:5, KJV). Now we are able to enter the kingdom of God when we become Christians at conversion. But Jesus says that we have to be born "of the Spirit" before we can do that. When Jesus talks about "born of water" here, the most likely interpretation of this is that he is referring to spiritual cleansing from sin, which Ezekiel prophesied when he said, "I will sprinkle clean water upon you, and you shall be clean from all your uncleanness, and from all your idols I will cleanse you. A new heart I will give you and a new spirit I will put within you" (Ezek. 36:25-26). Here the water symbolizes spiritual life that God will give. Ezekiel is prophesying that God will give an internal cleansing from the pollutions of sin in the heart at the same time as he awakens new spiritual life within his people. The fact that these two ideas are connected so closely in this well-known prophecy from Ezekiel, and the fact that Jesus assumes that Nicodemus should have understood this truth "are you a teacher of Israel, and yet you do not understand of this?" (John 3:10), together with the fact that throughout the conversation Jesus is talking about intensely spiritual concerns, all suggest that this is the most likely understanding of the passage. Another suggestion has been that "born of water" refers to physical birth and the "water" (amniotic fluid) that accompanies it, but it would hardly be necessary for Jesus to specify that one has to be born in this way when he is talking about spiritual birth, and it is questionable whether first-century Jews would have understood this phrase in this way. Another interpretation is that Jesus is referring to the water of baptism here, but baptism or any other similar ceremony is not in view in this passage (and it would have been anachronistic for Jesus to speak of Christian baptism here since that did not begin until Pentecost). Moreover, this would contradict the New Testament emphasis on the salvation by faith alone necessary for salvation, and something which, if it were true, we would certainly expect to find taught much more explicitly in the other New Testament passages that clearly deal with baptism.

Found in 1 John 3:9, John is explaining that whosoever is born of God both not commit sin, for his seed remaineth in him, and he cannot sin because he is born of God. His seed of life and generating and growing power within him, and that keeps the person living a life free of continual sin. This does not, of course, mean that the person will have a perfect life but only that the pattern of life will not be one of continuing indulgence in a sinful manner.

We should notice that John says this is true of everyone who is truly born again: "No one is born of God will continue to sin." Another way of looking at this is to say that "everyone who does what is right has been born of him" (John 2:29, KJV).

A divine, untainted Christ-like agape love will be in the results in a Christian life. "Everyone who loves has been born of God and knows God" (1 John 4:7 NIV). Mr. Grudem looks at other effects that indicate change (a new birth), which is the desire to overcoming the world, and his commands are not burdensome, for everyone born of God has overcome the world" (1 John 5:3-4 NIV). John explains that regeneration has given us the ability to overcome the daily pressures and temptations of the world that would otherwise have kept us in bondage and from being obedient to God's commandments and to remain on the right path of righteousness.

John identifies another result of regeneration, and that is to protect us from the attacks from Satan himself. "We know that anyone born of God does not continue to sin; the one was born of God and of Jesus will keep us safe, and the evil one cannot harm him" (1 John 5:18, NIV). Through with the permission from God there may be attacks from Satan, but John reassures God's children that "the one who is in you [us] is greater than the one who is in the world" (1 John 4:4, NIV). Praise God that his greater power of the Holy Spirit within us keeps us safe from any spiritual harm by the evil one.

We should be reminded that if there is genuine regeneration within a person's life, he or she will love his brother, will overcome the temptation of the world, and will be kept safe from any harm attempted by the tempter.

The Apostle Paul speaks of the "fruit of the Spirit." The result in life is produced by the power of the Holy Spirit working within every believer: "But the fruit of the Spirit is love, joy, peace, patience, kindness, goodness, faithfulness, gentleness, self-control" (Gal. 5:22-23, NIV). When one is truly regenerated, those elements of the fruits of the Spirit will be more and more prevalent in one's life, for unbelievers and for those who are pretenders will clearly lack character traits in their lives.

Jesus said in Matt. 7:15-20 for them to be aware of false prophets, who come to you in sheep's clothing but inwardly are ravenous wolves. You will know them by their fruits. Are grapes gathered from thorns, or figs from thistles? So, every sound tree bears good fruit, but the bad tree bears evil fruit. A sound tree cannot bear evil fruit, nor can a bad tree bear good fruit. Every tree that does not bear good fruit is cut down and thrown into the fire. Thus you will know them by their fruits.

Neither Jesus nor Paul nor John point to activity in the Church or miracles as evidence of regeneration. They rather point to the character traits in life. In fact, immediately after the verses quoted above, Jesus warns that on the Day of Judgment many will say to him, "Lord, Lord, did we not prophesy in your name, and cast out demons in your name, and do many mighty works in your name?" But he will declare to them, "I never knew you; depart from me, you evildoers" (Matt. 7:22-23).

But genuine love for God and his people, heartfelt obedience to his commands, and the Christians' character traits that Paul calls the fruit of the Spirit, demonstrated consistently over a period of time in a person's life, cannot be produced by Satan or by natural man or woman working in his own strength. Only can we be justified by the Spirit of God working within us, which produces and manifests a new life.

The question still remains: "Do you know Jesus?" Jesus was with God before the earth existed, left His glory with the Father and was born of a virgin, lived a perfect, sinless life, died on a Calvary cross for your redemption, and was raised again after three days. Today He is in heaven, and His sacrifice has provided a way for you and me to come to a saving faith. Being saved is fully a work of God. No one is saved by their own efforts. It is by grace alone, in faith alone, by Jesus alone; it is a gift of God (Eph. 2:8-9).

Just who is Jesus Christ? He is one of the most fascinating human figures in the history of mankind. As a member of the Trinity of God, the spirit of God humbles himself as the first son of a poor carpenter from the Judean countryside, which was occupied by the Roman Empire. It's recorded that he lived to reach the age of thirty-three. His ministry, which was a short three years, included his words and teachings, combined with his death on a cross by means of crucifixion. Jesus Christ became one of the greatest symbols of peace and the greatest fundamentalist religions that the world has ever seen.

We can identify three major branches of the Christian religion, such as Roman Catholicism, Protestantism, and Eastern Orthodoxy, which have certain perspectives on the theology of Jesus, and they all seem to agree that he did preach deep, involving messages about the salvation of mankind. His messages addressed the social and spiritual needs of the poor, of Jews' culture, and later on his relationship with the Gentiles. Jesus set the social services program in motion, providing the needs of the poor and those who are in need of healing, through his demonstration of pure love and genuine concerns. We see that today different races, cultures, and social classes come to adore him.

The uniqueness of Jesus was expressed by a quotation from a French military commander, Napoleon Bonaparte: "Between [Christ] and every other person in the world there is no possible term of comparison; Alexander, Caesar, Charlemagne, and I have founded empires. But on what did we rest the creation of our genius? Upon force. Jesus Christ founded His Empire upon love, and at this hour millions of men would die for Him."

This question of just "who was Jesus?" If John began to baptize in the fifteenth year of Tiberius Caesar (Luke 3:1), being A.D. 29, and if Jesus was thirty years of age when He was baptized, the traditional date fixed by Dionysius Exiguus would be approximately correct. But it is probable that the reign of Tiberius was reckoned by Luke from his admission to joint authority with Augustus in A.D. 1142, so that Jesus would be thirty in A.D. 25-6 and would be born about B.C. 5. This agrees with the representation of Matthew. That He was born under Herod, since Herod died B.C. 4, and a number of events of the infancy are mentioned as occurring before his death. Who He is remains unanswered and searched throughout the Christianity history. As a Christian, we believe that Jesus Christ is the second person of the Trinity, from glory, while in the presence of God, he announced, "I will go," and clothed himself with the flesh of a human over two thousand years ago. I announce in faith that he was born of a virgin. To my surprise, I have attended speeches by other religious leaders who believe that this event is impossible, that he was human male and a prophet. He was tempted but remained sinless during his life.

No account found in the book of Mark satisfactorily explains this omission if he knew of it, and seems incredible that, if known, it would not have been utilized in Pauline theology. Matthew and Luke themselves raise a grave difficulty, since the whole point of the genealogies seems to be that Jesus was descended from David through Joseph and is therefore David's heir.

The birth from a virgin was necessary to preserve Jesus from the cancer of the original sin committed by Adam and Eve. In the New Testament, God's words teach that Jesus was a real, historical person, who was born in Bethlehem (Matthew 2:1). He exhibited human characteristics of humanity such as being tired, hungry, thirsty, and having emotions, and his death was physical. The humanity of Jesus is one of the least controversial areas of Christology, but this was not always so. In the early centuries after Christ, some taught that Jesus' body suffering and death were merely appeared to be physical in nature. Scholars call this view "Docetism," from the Greek word meaning "to seem." Docetism arose from the gnostic worldview that all matter is evil and concluded that God could not have been associated with physicality.

Mary was truly His mother. An additional miracle must have been necessary to prevent the transmission of the cancer through her, and this subsidiary miracle could have safeguarded the sinlessness of Jesus without the miraculous conception.

Just who was Jesus Christ? Some called him the Messiah, the Hebrew word translated into English as "Messiah," means "anointed one." According to the Hebrew prophets, the Messiah is a king, which is a direct line from David, who would rescue Israel from her oppressors, return the motherland, Jerusalem, back into the hands of the Jewish people, and bring in the Spirit of Peace. The Jews believe that Jesus did not accomplish these prophecies that other Christians believe he has.

The New Testament equivalent of the term "Messiah" is "Christ Jesus," so the New Testament title "Christ" signifies that Jesus' followers believe he is the Messiah. Affirmations of Jesus as the Messiah are found in abundance in the four Gospel narratives and the Acts of the Apostles. Found in the Pauline and other epistles, many of which predate the Gospel, also attempt to show that Jesus is the Messiah, yet they refer to him almost exclusively as "Christ"!

In the four Gospels, we find others and Jesus himself to identify himself as being the Messiah. Found in John 1:41, Jesus, after meeting Andrew, who ran to tell Peter that he had found the Messiah. At the well, Jesus has a conversation with the Samaritan woman. She replied that she knew the Messiah was coming. Jesus replies, "I who speak to you am he"(John 4:25-26). In Matthew 16:16; Mark 8:29; Luke 9:20, Jesus asks his disciples who they think he is, and Peter answers and proclaims, "You are the Christ." "Hosanna to the Son of David!" was a song of praise as we see Jesus' triumphal entry. This act fulfilled the prophecy of Zechariah 9:9 and Matthew 21:4-9. When our redeemer stands trial before the Sanhedrin, the high priest asks him if he is "the Christ, the Son of the Blessed One." Jesus replied, "I am" (Mark 14:61-62).

Just who was Jesus? Jesus was the Son of Man; "the Son of Man" has been used eighty-one times in the Gospels, and always by Jesus. Who else but Jesus could have used the term? Biblical scholars turn to its use in the Old Testament. There the term "Son of Man" is used in three main contexts: first, to address to the prophet Ezekiel (Ezekiel 2:1), and second, to refer to humanity in general, especially its lowliness when compared to God and the angels (Numbers 23:19), (Psalm 8:14), and lastly to refer to an eschatological figure whose coming signals the end of times (Daniel 7:13-14).

We have identified Jesus as being divinely named "The Messiah, the Word of God, the Son of Man." Jesus is also called the Son of God. The disciples' experience of Jesus of Nazareth was such that the attributes of Yahweh came readily to their minds as they attempted to understand that experience and communicate it to others under the guidance of the Holy Spirit. This led them to speak of Jesus as Lord and God in those same terms that were used to describe Yahweh in the Old Testament. "Jesus is Yahweh, Lord" (kurios Iesous) became one of the earliest confessional formulas of the Church, and its utterance was specifically credited to inspiration by the Holy Spirit (1 Cor. 12:3).

Jesus is God; we find in scripture of the Old Testament and the New Testament verses, such as written by the Apostle John (John 1:1,14). In the beginning was the Word, and the Word was with God, and the Word was God. The Word became flesh and made his dwelling among us. Thomas said to him, "My Lord and my God!" (John 20:28). But about the Son he, God, says, "Your throne, O God, will last forever and ever" (Hebrews 1:8).

Some important titles and functions applied to Christ in the New Testament indicate early belief in his divinity. The Statement "Jesus Christ is Lord (Greek kyrious, Hebrew adonat)" is found throughout the New Testament and was one of the earliest Christian confessions of faith.

Noted by Alister McGrath, the New Testament writers apply the following functions to Jesus that are associated with God. Jesus is the Savior of humanity (Matthew 1:21, Acts 4:12, Luke 2:11). It is appropriate to call on the name of Jesus in prayer (1 Car. 1:2) and to worship him (Matthew 28:9), and finally Jesus reveals God directly: "Anyone who has seen me has seen the Father" (John 14:9).

Today Jesus has been given many different attributes, and we identify with Him in a more personal manner. Individuals in times of despair pray unto Jesus for His Peace (John 14:27). Found in the King James Version, we read: "Peace I leave with you, my peace I give unto you: not as the world giveth, give I unto you. Let not your heart be troubled, neither let it be afraid."

When I go through the many storms of life, I am convinced that through my faith in Jesus he will restore my peace. In a short testimony of Michael Jones, we can witness the grace of God as Michael's story has become a common story of today's African-American society. His story topic is titled "That Getting-Up Stuff." I really can't think of anything in particular that I have done to cause tragedy to strike my life the way it did. I was going about my life, in a daily routine, and tending to my personal affairs, when suddenly a series of tragedies struck my family. Then tragedy struck my physical body, leaving me unconscious in a hospital, with three bullets lodged in me.

Prior to the tragedies, from the time he was sixteen or seventeen years old, he had been attending Trinity United Church of Christ in Chicago. Two African-American men whom he admired attended that church, so he followed their examples: his uncle, Reverend Reginald Johnson, and Officer James Rivers, who lived across the street. He was attending church about once a month in those days. He was also attending Chicago State University, studying accounting.

Out of college, he began working in a flower shop, which was owned by his church. It seems that God placed a hedge of protections surrounding men and women of God who became role models for him to emulate. He worked there four years before the closure of the flower shop. He was hired as a custodian at the church and developed a strong relationship with one of the female preachers and her family. As he was working God was working on him, calling him for services. He finally believed that Christ was for him and felt he had no reasons to continue to shy away from Him anymore. After becoming an heir in the Kingdom of God, it seemed that everything was going smoothly.

Saints of God, when times are going smoothly surrounding you, it's time to place on your full armor of God. Shine and polish every item, begin to fast and pray, because Satan has seen the wonderful relationship that is developing between you and God. He becomes jealous. He asked God permission to test your faith in Him. He will bring about pain, death, stripping all you value, and even loss of job.

Satan first attacked, caused tragedy, and attacked his family by the death of his grandfather, secondly the loss of uncle, then a cousin was kidnapped and killed, and finally his mother was called home. He recalled not understanding how God could take the most important people in his life away. Found in the book of Job, we read that even Job addressed the same questions to God: "Why?"—a question that will be asked throughout the history of Christianity. But God was not finished with him yet; He had to draw him closer to him because a second cousin had been kidnapped. Satan attacked Him through his thoughts. He would not allow the death of his cousin be like the first, so he began to search for his cousin. One day he spotted his cousin's van and approached it, and he was shot three times by the driver sitting in the van. "Drew me closer." While in the hospital, he was visited by the ministry staff from his church, and he recalled seeing the Father, the Son, and the Holy Ghost holding his hands while they were in prayer. There in the hospital, his prayers were continued. He felt a closeness to God. After being released from the hospital, he went back to working at the church, where the peace of Jesus surrounds him.

The Cross
A symbol of my faith that strengthens me each day
As I by God's grace walk the narrow way!
You see God's own Son He gave His life for me
and took my debt of sin
To a place called Calvary.
Own Him my life and all I'll ever be
All He asks is that I'll let Him live through me.
So I run the race Empowered by His grace and give Him all the glory

As I look into His face.
Jesus is LORD!

The happy state that the final results while knowing and serving the only living God. A number of Greek and Hebrew words are used in the Bible to convey the ideas of joy and rejoicing. We have the same situation in the English with such nearly synonymous words as joy, happiness, pleasure, delight, gladness, merriment, felicity, and enjoyment. The words "joy" and "rejoice" are the words used most often to translate the Hebrew and Greek words into English. "Joy" is found over one hundred fifty times in the Bible. If such words as "joyous" and "joyful" are included, the number comes to over two hundred. The verb "rejoices" appears well over two hundred times.

Joy is the fruit of a right relationship with God. It is not something people can create by their efforts. The Bible distinguishes joy from pleasure. The Greek word for "pleasure" is the word from which we get our word "hedonism," the philosophy of self-centered pleasure-seeking. Paul referred to false teachers as "lovers of pleasures more than lovers of God" (2 Timothy 3:4). The Bible warns that self-indulgent pleasure-seeking does not lead to happiness and fulfillment. Ecclesiastes 2:1-11 records the sad testimony of one who sought to build his life on pleasure-seeking. The search left him empty and disillusioned. Proverbs 14:13 offers insight into this way of life: "Even in laughter the heart is sorrowful." Cares, riches, and pleasure rob people of the possibility of fruitful living (Luke 8:14). Pleasure-seeking often enslaves people in a vicious cycle of addiction (Titus 3:3). The self-indulgent person, according to 1 Timothy 5:6, is dead while seeming still to be alive.

Many people think that God is the killjoy. Nothing could be a bigger lie. God Himself knows joy, and He wants his people to know, experience, joy. Psalm 104:31 speaks of God Himself rejoicing in His creative works. Isaiah 65:18 speaks of God rejoicing over His redeemed people, who will be to Him "a joy." Praise God.

My brothers and sisters, the question still remains: "Do you know Jesus?" Found in Luke 10:21, we find the words of God that express the joy of Jesus, another experience we share with our redeemer. In that hour I rejoiced in spirit and said, "I thank thee, O Father, Lord of heaven and earth, that thou hast hid these things from the wise and prudent, and hast revealed them unto babes: even so, Father; for so it seemed good in thy sight" (Luke 10:21, KJV).

In that hour, Jesus rejoiced in spirit. More than "rejoiced"; the Greek word "rather" signifies "exulted." Very rarely in the holy story of the lives is a hint given us of any gleam of gladness of the joy irradiating the spirit of the man of sorrow. The exultation of the blessed here was based his conviction that this first success of his own was but the commencement of a long and weary, but yet, in the end, of a triumphant campaign against the spirit of sin and evil. Dr. Plumpte continues to search a new paradigm, which causes change in and through the mortal weakness by the aid of their poor, imperfect faith in His name (Jesus). He was able to accomplish, was an earnest, a pledge, of the mighty works, which his followers would, in the power of the same name, be enabled to effect in the coming ages. In the solemn hour did the Messiah see, in the far future, of "the travail of his soul," and was satisfied. The absence of all signs of joy in the life of our Lord is well brought out in that touching legend, which we find in the spurious letter of Paul's luntulus to the senate, that he wept often but that no one had ever seen him smile.

In the Bible we find a written story of the woman who comes into the synagogue (Luke 13:10-17). Jesus healed a woman of an ailment. When Jesus met this woman, she was bent over with a spirit of weakness. It is important to focus on the word "spirit," because healings are spiritual as well as physical. Recall that Jesus said it was a spirit that had crippled this woman for eighteen years. The woman was bound by Satan. However, Jesus set her free.

The story of the woman is particularly significant because in the synagogue, women were not allowed in the center, particularly within worship spaces. Usually, they remained in the back, within the outer courtyards. Christ not only brought her into the center but, following her healing, she praised God there. That is, Jesus liberated this woman to do what only men of her time were allowed to do. Jesus took the initiative and called her into the center.

Before this woman could even experience the joy of healing, Jesus turned the faces of present and forced them again to question the law that contained their bondage. Jesus confronted a system of domination, which had allowed women access to God only through males. Jesus demonstrated that the only domination He supported was the domination of God. Jesus was against the oppression that caused this woman to have a weak spirit. He was against sexism, satanic domination, and the spirit of weakness that was in this woman.

Jesus heals people or casts out demons. There would not be much narrative left. Jesus reached out, not only to this woman, who was not allowed worship space in the temple, but to lepers, tax collectors, and others victims of oppressive systems. In His healing, he inhaled and exhaled a second name, a new name, a new title, one that doesn't occur anywhere else in the Bible: "Daughter of Abraham." The term "Son of Abraham" was a common Biblical title, which carried among the males a badge of honor.

In naming her "Daughter of Abraham," Jesus said to her and the world, "You don't have to have a husband to be a special relative of God. You don't have to have a son. You don't have to have a father. You are somebody as a daughter. That is the only connection you need. You are a 'Daughter of Abraham.' With that connection, you have direct kinship to God."

Then imagine yourself like this woman, walking down a dusty street, slipping into the back of a synagogue unobtrusively so that no one would push you away. Imagine yourself praying from your heart that God would release you from eighteen years of bondage. Then without your knowing it, Jesus comes into the room. He looks over the crowd to where you are and calls you to come to Him. Then Jesus has a word for you. He says, "You are free!" That announcement is for everyone who is reading this dissertation, no matter the situation.

Jesus can set you free from your ailments. "What joy and peace we find in Jesus." "Praise God."

Jesus demonstrated a love that is unmatched, a love that is pure and unreflective.

⋘◇⋙

Only Jesus

Only Jesus can make a sad heart glad,
the only one who can give the best joy you ever had
He fills the hungry heart to satisfied and full,
the only one who can redeem the sinful soul
Only Jesus can wash sins away,

the only one who can turn the night into day
He will always say "I forgive you"
the only one who can change a heart to make it new
Only Jesus can comfort you when need a friend,
the only one who stays with you to the end
He is always on duty caring for his sheep,
the only one who loves so tenderly and deep
Only Jesus can heal a broken heart,
the only one who shares our sorrows and takes a part
He is the Savior, who knows our deepest woes,
the only one who gives victory over all our foes.
Only Jesus can dry away our tears,
the only one who calms all our fears
He is always there to strengthen in times of need,
the only one to follow as he does guide and lead
Only Jesus can see the lonesome heart and void
the only one who can fill it to overjoyed
He is always there to hear our pleadings and request,
the only one who gives perfect peace and rest.

A Christian poem by Cindy Wyatt

"These things have I spoken unto you, that my joy might remain in you, and that your joy might be full." (John 15:11).

Jesus first loved you. This is why you should love Him. The Word of God that stepped out of ranks when God called for a volunteer, and He announced to His Father, "I will go." His love for his Father and the love that He holds for his creations caused Him to stand for salvation. Only through his blood we find the cleansing power, strong enough to wash away our sins. The Son of God's (Jesus') love is poured out of the windows of heaven, showering on the just as well as the unjust. Only through the acceptances of Jesus can we come into the presence of God. Only through the redeeming power of His blood can we sit at the table of grace. I love Him because He first loved me.

Dr. G. G. Findlay provides definition of the word "love" found in the Hasting Dictionary of the Bible, from a spiritual point of view. If love to God is rekindled by the knowledge of God's love to man in Christ, this holds no less of man's love to man, to which most New Testament instances of the word refer. This matter of the second commandment of Jesus, which is like unto the first and is grounded equally with it upon creation and the true order of the world.

Sins brought in by Satan, spreading of hate, lusting for physical and material items, deceit, the death of love and life in our human nature. In laying down his life for us, Jesus Christ has laid the foundation of a new empire of love, a regime and fashion of life the opposite of that inaugurated by Cain.

The new commandment is, after all, the old commandment, which men had from the beginning. God's Fatherly love manifests in the unstinted bounties of nature, which visits the just and unjust every day and dictates to His children to love his enemies and kindness to the evil ones.

The love of Christ reaffirming and immensely reinforcing the primeval law constrains us to live no longer to ourselves but to Him (2 Co. 5:14-19) in living to Him lives for His Church and for humanity (Eph. 3:3-9). If a man says "I love God" and hates his brother, he is a liar (John 2:9). The terms of Christ's redemption bind His witnesses and engage parties to God's covenant of grace in Christ made with mankind (John 1:29; John 6:33). The gift of the spirit is bestowed expressly with this world aim in view; the salvation of each sinner is a step toward an earnest of the world's salvation (Matthew 5:13). The love of God must reach the world and rule the world through those who know it in knowing the grace of our Lord Jesus.

"That if thou shalt confess with thy mouth the Lord Jesus, and shalt believe in thine heart that hath raised him from the dead, thou shalt be saved" (Romans 10:9, KJV).

⋙⋘

Jesus Is Everything

My Father My redeemer, Prince of Peace
My Savior My Shepherd, You are all I need
My Joy My Salvation, King, Lamb and Light

I pray today and cling to you
Please see me pure in your sight
Please wash me clean with your precious blood
And rid me of all past sin, I accept you as my everything
So let this love begin, and now I vow to always try my very best with You
I hope dear Lord I make you proud
It's all I want to do
And if by chance I look away for not a second more
You'd gently lead me back to this great Love
that I adore
By Angie

⬥

Conclusion

The breath of regeneration is the breath of God, the same breath that He used to bring forward the words of creation. The same breath that he used to end His workday: "It is good." He who announced placing the stars in the heaven, fish in the seas, the crowing insect on the ground, green vegetation, the sun to rule in the day, and the moon to rule at night, ensuring there was physical light to help govern the days and nights, and introduced the coming of the seasons. His spoken Word, with the help of the Holy Spirit, together created male and female in their image and gave instructions to go forth and multiply. "It was good." And He rested on the sixth day.

This is the same breath that was forced into the nostril of a molded shape of a man formed from the dust of an earth in the image of God. Both Adam and Eve were created for the sole purpose to worship God and work in the Garden of Eden, but there they were influenced by the fallen angel from heaven, Satan. His cunning and crafty attitude persuaded Adam and Eve to become disobedient to the Word of God, which caused the first sin.

The breath of God mixed with the assistance of the Holy Ghost conducted regeneration sovereign work, which was predicted in the Old Testament prophecy of Ezekiel. God promised a time would come when he would give new spiritual life to his people:

"A new heart I will give you, and a new spirit I will put within you; and I will take out of you flesh the heart of stone and give you a heart of the flesh.

And I will put my spirit within you, and cause you to walk in my statutes and be careful to observe my ordinances" (Ezek. 36:26-27).

God's loving breath, His soft and pleasing voice, still remain in the wind throughout world even today, calling his chosen children for salvation. God's invitations to discipleship are still being given out to those who remain eligible, ready to accept the saving grace through our redeemer, Jesus Christ.

The divine breath of God was given by God to his children to help restore, to guide, to bring back into remembrance those things spoken to them throughout their life. Adam and Eve, who reside in Paradise with our Creator, fell short of the mark and began a distractive lifecycle for all mankind, yet Adam and Eve still remained under the grace of God.

Today, with the help of the Holy Spirit, we can accept with faith and truth of Jesus' birth, teaching, death, resurrection, and ascension into heaven, the Word of God (Jesus Christ) has redeemed us from the curse of disobedience of the first sin made by our first parents.

When establishing a new or reconstructing a falling relationship with Jesus, we have to yell a remorsefully, repetitive heart. As a baby in Christ Jesus, He provides you with the milk that contains a mixture of nutrition to help strengthen your spiritual level of growth. As a member of the house of God who has fallen down, you still remain in the grace of God. He will extend his hand to support you as he gives you instructions to stand. During this period of reconstruction, we have to be sincere in our attitude for repentance of our sins. These are some of the steps when asking God forgiveness of the sins. For those who remain eligible for baptism in water, a confession of your sins, and those who realized their desperate need for the Savior, He will open His doors to a renewal salvation.

Salvation contains a "yes-type attitude." Develop a loving belief that Jesus is your personal Savior, a belief that requires your heart and not your mind. Rely on, fully trusting in the words of God, leaning on the Word of God and resting in his word. Believing with all your heart that Jesus is your Savior first and the healing of the Holy Spirit will help you to make strong connections to Jesus. There is no other way to the Father in heaven except by Jesus Christ alone.

When God is calling out the names of those who remain eligible for salvation, he is breathing on us. This action places into the air His spirit and places in us a newness, a new spirit that helps fill our minds with a desire to want more understanding. Through God's grace, we can ask for more wisdom and a stronger faith and be more dependent on those things. Hope for an everlasting trust in the Word of God, through our redeemer, Jesus Christ.

In the article written by Mr. Jack Wellman titled "What Is the Bible Definition of Wisdom? How Are We Wise in God's Eyes?" he points out three factors that wisdom is not intelligence or knowledge or even understanding. He identifies those as something we use to think or act in a way that common sense prevails, and choices are beneficial and productive. I am in agreement with him that we can't get wisdom out of a textbook. We can't get knowledge enough to make you wise and through understanding from just hearing others. Experience might be one of the most valuable tools in acquiring wisdom. What we learn from experience gives us the wisdom, whether to try a particular thing or make a certain choice or not.

From the Bible we find a different definition of the word "wisdom." Found in Proverbs 9:10: "The fear of the Lord is the beginning of wisdom: and the knowledge of the holy is understanding." The word "fear," which is used quite often today due to the terrorist activities around the world, has meaning to those who are affected directly or through the fast means of broadcasting news with such speed effects in the whole world. Fear is identified by The Holman Illustrated Bible Dictionary as fear is a natural emotional response to a perceived threat to one's security or general welfare. It ranges in degree of intensity from a sense of anxiety or worry to one of utter terror. It can be a useful emotion when it leads to appropriate caution or measures that would guard one's welfare. On the other hand, fear can be a hindrance to the enjoyment of life if it is induced by delusion or if it lingers and overpowers other more positive emotions such as love and joy, perhaps leading to an inability to engage in the normal activities of life. In the Bible, fear is perhaps more often than in popular culture regarded not as pure emotion but as wise behavior.

Real wisdom is the fear of God; there are three basic definitions of wisdom summarizing the status of the field of study very well. The first, wisdom is considered by many to be simply the art of learning how to succeed in life. Apparently ancient persons learned very early that there was orderliness to the world in which they lived. They also learned in accordance with that orderliness (Prov. 22:17-24:22). Second, wisdom is considered by some to be a philosophical study of the essence of life. Certainly much of the books of Job and

Ecclesiastes seem to deal with just such existential issues of life (Job 30:29-31). Third, though the other definitions might include this, it seems that the real essence of wisdom is spirit, for life is more than just living by a set of rules and being rewarded in some physical manner. Undoubtedly, "thanks be to God."

This sense of wisdom comes from God (Prov. 2:6). It really begins with God and one's faith in Him as Lord and Savior (Prov. 1:7; Job 28:28).

The fear of God induces wisdom, and through wisdom we see that one's faith in God is a needed ingredient (Hebrews 11:1). Now faith is the substance of things hoped for, the evidence of things not seen (Ephesians 1:17), that the God of our Lord Jesus Christ, the Father of glory, may give unto you the spirit of wisdom and revelation in the knowledge of him. The concept of faith has been radically redefined in some philosophical and theological circles during the past century. Throughout the scripture, faith is the trustful human response to God's self-revelation via His words and His actions. God initiates the relationship between Himself and human beings. He expects people to trust Him; failure to trust Him was in essence the first sin (Gen. 3:17). Since the fall of humanity, God nurtures and inspires trust in Him through what He says and does for the benefit of people who need Him.

Jesus was with God before the earth exited, left His glory with the Father, and was born of a virgin, lived a perfect, sinless life, died on Calvary for your redemption, and was raised again after three days. Today He is in heaven, and His sacrifice has provided a way for you to find salvation only with faith. Being saved is fully a work of God. No one is saved by his or her works. No one is saved by their own efforts. It is by the grace alone, in faith alone, by Jesus alone. It is a gift of God (Eph. 2:8-9). We pray that you will come to believe in Jesus Christ, be born again, and be saved right now.

The power of prayer: Dear Father in heaven, I thank you for all the good things that you have bestowed upon me, especially for the precious gift of life. Thank you for having so loved the world that you sent to us your divine Son, Jesus Christ, who died on the cross for our salvation.

Jesus, my Savior and best Friend, grant to me and those who are dear to me the blessings of good health, both of mind and body. Help me to do your holy will in all things. May I love my neighbor as myself, ever seeing in him the reflection of your face.

I believe that in God there are three Divine Persons: Father, Son, and Holy Spirit. I believe that God in His mercy and justice rewards goodness and punishes evil.

For all the sins of my life, I am truly sorry, Dear Lord, because they have offended you, who is goodness itself. I love you with all my heart, and with your help I will try never to offend you again. Assist me to do all that is necessary to obtain eternal life.

When the trials and temptations of this world press heavily upon my heart, walk beside and in me, Good Shepherd, and I shall fear no evil. Have mercy on me, Lord, and hear my prayer. Amen.

Only through the acceptance of Jesus Christ is the only way we can have the eternal life with our Lord and Savior Jesus. Peace, Lord, make me an instrument of thy peace. Where there is hate, let me sow love; where there is injury, pardon; where there is doubt, faith; where there is despair, hope; where there is darkness, light; and where there is sadness, joy.

Divine Master, grant that I may not so much seek to be consoled as to console, to be loved as to love, for it is in giving that we receive, it is in pardoning that we are pardoned, and it is in dying that we are born to eternal life.

BIBLIOGRAPHY

1. Allen, David and Shartt A. David. *Basic Studies in Soteriology.* Xulon Press. Printed in the United States of America, 2005.

2. Banks, Sr. Melvin E. LITF.D. and Ogbonnaya, PH.D.Okechukwcu A. *Celebrate the Gospel of Jesus* by; Publisher Urban Ministries, Inc. Chicago, IL 60643-6987, 2000

3. Barclay, William *The Parables of Jesus* Westminster John Knox Press, Louisville, 1970 4. Barackman, Floyd H. *Practical Christian Theology* By; Kregel Publications, a Division of Kregel Inc., Grand Rapids, MI 49501, 2012

5. Beck, Harrell F. *Our Biblical Heritage* By; the Division of Christian Education and the Division of Publication of the United Church Board for Homeland Ministries, 1964

6. Blackaby, Henry T. and Brandt, Henry *The Power of the Call* By; Printed in the United State of America, 1997

7. Blanch, Stuart *Living by Faith* by; William B. Eerdmans Publishing Company Grand Rapids, Michigan, 1984

8 .Brumby, W. Clayton *The Missing Ministry, Recapturing Church Growth through effective Church Sian Evangelism* By; W. Clayton Brumby, Sarasota, FL 34239, 1998

9. Cairns, D. S.; Smith, Richard R. *The Faith That Rebels* by; permission of Harper & Brothers, NY, 1930

10. Chambers, Oswald *My Utmost for His Highest* By; Oswald chambers Pub-

lications Association, Ltd. Grand Rapids, Michigan, 1992

11. Creek, Humble *Light for My Path, Illuminating Selections from the Bible* by; Barbour Publishing, Inc. Humble Creek, Uhrichsville, Ohio 44683, 1996

12. Davenport, Russell *The Dignity of Man* by: permission of Harper & Brothers; NY 1955

13. Delumeaau, Jean and Matthew O'Connell *History of Paradise, The Garden of Eden in Myth and Tradition* By; University of Illinois Press, 2000

14. DeHaan, Richard W. *Your Pastor and You* By; Thomas Nelson, Inc., Grand Rapids, MI. Printed in USA, 1982

15. Geisler, Norman L. Christian Apologetics By; Baker Academic Publishing Group Grand Rapids, Michigan, 1976

16. Gifford, Millard M. *Make It Beautiful* By; Vantage Press, Inc. New York, NY, 1979

17. Grenz, Stanley J. *Theology for the Community of God* BY; Broadman and Holman Publishers, Nashville, Tennessee, 1994

18. Grier, William H. M.D. and Cobbs, Price M. M. D. *The Jesus Bag* By; McGraw-Hill Book Company, New York, 1971

19. Gustafson, James M. *Theology and Christian Ethics* by: A Pilgrim Press Book, from the United Church Press, Philadelphia, 1974

20. Grudem, Wayne Systemic *Theology: An Introduction To Biblical Doctrine* by: Zondervan, Grand Rapids, Michigan 2000 21 .*The New Interpreter's Study Bible* By; Abingdon Press, Nashville, TN 37202, 1989

22. Harrison, Everett F. *A Short Life of Christ* By; WM. B. Publishing Company Grand Rapids, Michigan 1968

23. Lacocque, Andre *The Trail of Innocence, Adam and Eve and the Yahwist* By; Wipf and Stock Publisher, 2006

24. Marshall, Catherine *Beyond Our Selves* by: McGraw Hill Book Company, Inc. New York Toronto London, 1961

25. Meyers, David John *The Illustrated Life of Jesus* By Hylas Published Irvington, New York 10533, 2005

26. .McGrath, Alister E. Christian *Theology An Introduction* By; Blackwell Publishers Inc., Massachusetts 02148, 1997

27. Motyer, Alec *The Story of the Old Testament* By; Baker Book House Company Grand Rapids, MI 49516-6287, 2001

28. Morris, Henry, Ill After Eden *Understand Creation, The Curse, and the Cross*

By Master Book, 2003

29. Nickelson, Ronald L. *Standard Lesson Commentary* By; Standard Publishing Cincinnati, Ohio, 2008

30. Williams, J.B. Matthew *Henry's Commentary* By; Hendricks Publishers, Inc. Printed in the United States, 2006

31. Schaper, Robert N. *In His Presence* By; Thomas Nelson Publishers, New York, 1984

32. Shirer, Priscilla E. *A Jewel In His Crown* By; Moody Press, Chicago, III, 60610, 1999

33. Stanley, Charles *Experiencing Forgiveness* By; Thomas Nelson Publishers, Nashville Tn. 1996

34. *The Church of Yahweh The Breath of God 1996-2010;* http://www.yhwh.com/cross/cross20.htm

35. Jung, C. G. *Modern Man in Search of a Soul* by: permission of Harcourt, Bruce and World, Inc., and Routledge and Kegan Paul, Ltd.

36. Dickerson, Roy E. and Kunkel, Fritz *How Character Develops* by: permission of Charles Scribner's Sons

37. Lewis, C. S. *Beyond Personality* by: permission of the Macmillan Company and Geoffrey Bles, Ltd.

38. Moffat, James *The Bible* by: A New Translation, Harper & Brothers 1950

Dake, Jennings F. Dake's Annotated Reference Bible: The Holy Bible by: Dake Publishing, Inc. Lawrenceville, Ga. 2014

39, *Holman Christian Standard Bible* by: Holman Bible Publishers 2009

40. Prescott, Margaret, *Montague Twenty Minutes of Reality* by: Atlantic Monthly Company, Inc. Boston, Massachusetts 1916

41. Oursler, Fulton *Why I Know There Is a God,* by: Doubleday & Company Inc. Mrs. April Armstrong, 1950

42. Phillips, J. B., *The Gospels Translated into Modern English* by: permission Macmillan Company and Geoffrey Bles, Ltd.

43. Simpson, A. B. *The Gospel of Healing* by: Christian Publishing, Harrisburg, Pa. 1935

44. Hastings, James D.D *Dictionary Of The Bible* by: Charles Scribner's Sons, NY 1909, 1989

45. Cowman, L. B. *Streams In The Desert: 366 Daily Devotional Readings* by: Zondervan Publishing House 1996

46. Henry's, Matthew, *Matthew Henry's Commentary On The Whole Bible* by: Hendricks Publishing, Inc. Printed in the United States of America, 2006

47. Found, James; Olson, Bruce MDiv. *Basic Greek: In 30 Minutes A Day* by: Bethany House, Minneapolis, Minnesota 1983

48. Wilson, Sandra D. Into *Abba's Arms: Finding Acceptance You've Always Wanted* by: Tyndale House Publishing, Inc. Carol Stream, Illinois 1998

49. Barnhart, Phil *Seasoning For Sermons* by: The C.S.S. Publishing Company, Inc. 1084

50. Wheeler, Raiford S. Rev. Dr. *A View From The Parsonage* by:Xulon Press, Printed In the United States Of America, 2012

51. Crrossan, John Dominic *The Greatest Prayer: Rediscovering the Revolutionary Message of the Lord's Prayer* by: Harper Collins Publishing, 2010

52. Scazzero, Peter; Bird, Warren, Ford, Leighton *The Emotionally Healthy Church* by: Zondervan, Grand Rapids, Michigan 2010

53. Vine, W. E.; Unger, Merrill F.; White, William Jr. Vine's *Expository Dictionary of Biblical Words* by: Thomas Nelson Publishers, Nashville, Camden, New York 1985

54. *He Breathed on them; www.theopologetic.com/2012/04/01/he-breahed-on-them 2012*

55. Schurig, Stefan *World Future Council: Hamburg; Regenerative Urban Development: A Roadmap to the City we need* by: www.futureofcitiesforum.com 2013

56. *Gifts of the Holy Spirit* http://faithfirst.com/RCLsacraments/confirmationteens/older/gifts spitit.html

57. Jackson, Wayne *What Is the "Gift of the Holy Spirit" in Acts 2:38* by: www.christiancourier.com/artica1/715 12/02/2014

58. Torrey, R. A. The *Regenerating Work of the holy Spirit: The Person and Work of the Holy Spirit* http://Biblehub.com 12/02/2014

59. King James Version *Amplified Bible Old & New Testament* by: Zondervan Grand Rapids, Michigan 1995

60. Paul, Leslie *Son of Man: The Life of Christ* by: E. P. Dutton & Co., Inc. New York 1961

61. Strom, Linda; Meeuwsen, Terry *Karla Faye Tucker: Set Free; Life & Faith on Death Row* by: WaterBrook Press; Colorado Springs, Colorado 2006

62. Banks, Melvin E. Sr. Litt.D. ; Ogbonnaya, Okechukwu, A. Ph.D. *Celebrate*

the Gospel of Jesus by: Leader's Guide; Urban Ministries, Inc., Chicago, II 2000

63. Blanch, Stuart *Living by Faith* by: William B. Eerdmans Publishing Company Grand Rapids, Michigan 1983

64. White, Randy; Bakke, Ray *Encounter God in the City* by: InterVarsity press, Downers Grove, Illinois 2006

65. Barackman, Floyd H. *Practical Christian Theology* by:Kregel Publications Inc., Grand Rapids, MI 2012